Help, God! I'm Broke!

Help, God! I'm Broke!

**Leave lack behind and
step into miraculous provision**

by Patricia King

Published by XP Publishing
A department of Christian Services Association
P.O. Box 1017
Maricopa, Arizona 85139
www.XPpublishing.com

ISBN-13: 978-1-936101-33-7
ISBN-10: 1-936101-33-5

Written in Honor of
Jehovah Jireh — the Lord who Provides

Thank You, Jesus,
for being constantly faithful
and forever good!

ENDORSEMENTS

Position yourself for the great transfer of wealth that God is bestowing upon believers, even in the midst of economic shaking. Through the pages of this book, be equipped with Kingdom economic principles that will release miraculous provision in your life.

CHÉ AHN
Senior Pastor, HRock Church
President, Harvest International Ministry

Patricia King is one of the most generous individuals I know. Her testimony of overcoming poverty and living in Kingdom provision will take you closer to the heart of what God intends for all of His children. This book is a MUST READ for the challenging economic climate we face in this hour.

STACEY CAMPBELL
www.revivalnow.com
www.beahero.org

Our first-ever Elijah List speaker at our first-ever Elijah List conference was Patricia King. I've watched her in real life. I've heard her real stories. When she ministered on the Elijah List cruise with our team, she couldn't wait to get off the ship and evangelize people on the islands. So when Patricia writes anything or talks about ANY subject, she has my ear! Please read this book if you have need of a financial breakthrough. It will help you. I promise!

STEVE SHULTZ
The Elijah List

I had a blast reading this book! In typical anointed Patricia King style, she is bringing the body of Christ up a level with amazing testimonies, insights loaded with wisdom and practical steps on how to break out of lack and into Kingdom abundance. I loved every word and was personally encouraged and challenged − I believe you will be, too. Dive in and get ready to be taken up a level in faith!

FAYTENE KRYSKOW
Revivalist
Leader of TheCRY/MY Canada

As I began reading the chapters in Patricia King's new book *Help, God − I'm Broke,* I was SO encouraged. I love the personal stories because I could see my own story within some of these stories. This book is also packed with Scripture. I found myself deep in intercession for my own finances right in the middle of her chapters and then filled with a new faith that God has a plan for my finances. He cares about everything that we care about. I love that about our God. This one line became written on my heart: "Blessings of abundance are looking for you. They want to catch you. They want to 'get you.'"

I encourage you to get this book, pray these Scriptures and watch God break out in the midst of your finances.

JULIE MEYER
International House Of Prayer – KC

My first reaction to this title was that the book would certainly fit a lot of hurting people today who are exactly in that position. As I read the book, my reaction changed to awareness that it was full of principles which fit everyone's life.

Before I finished it I became aware of something building inside of me. Was it the excitement of "hearing" the testimonies of miraculous intervention of so many who called out for help, the thought that angels were actually being sent to minister on my behalf, or hope for so many who are hurting financially? Of course it was all of these, but something more than emotion was happening. It was faith laying hold of direction.

I have lived by faith all my life and seen God provide always, but this was more than being about me, it was like a special word from God for this season for all.

You will not only be blessed in reading Patricia's latest book, you will be equipped to never again have to pray, "Help, God – I'm broke."

By applying the truths she shares, you will simply pray, "Help, God," and He will. I heartily recommend this book to the poor and the prosperous.

IVERNA TOMPKINS, DD

Every believer should take the time to read Patricia King's new book, *Help, God, I'm Broke.* It is much more than just another book about finances, it is the victorious testimony of God's faithfulness to her life, ministry and family for decades.

Patricia beautifully blends her and other's testimonies with a wealth of insightful biblical teaching and practical steps of action for financial blessing. I've had the privilege of being Patricia and Ron's pastor for the past few years.

Patricia is one of the most loving and giving people I've ever met. She lives what she teaches and so can you as you read and put into practice the principles she shares in this very timely book.

PASTOR MICHAEL MAIDEN
Church For The Nations

Do you want the power and ability to excel and prosper financially so you can fulfill your Kingdom assignment? Then this book is for you! Patricia shares not only her own personal life journey into financial blessing, but also gives both supernatural and natural keys for you to obtain your financial breakthrough. You will learn how to dispatch angels, war in the Spirit, receive supernatural provision, as well as create a budget, establish a balanced lifestyle of blessing and productivity, and much more! I highly recommend *Help, God*

– I'm Broke, if you want to get un-broke and move forward into a life of financial blessing and abundance.

MATT SORGER
Host of Power for Life
Matt Sorger Ministries

Filled with true life testimonies, Scripture references and practical keys to unlock the provision of God, *Help, God, I'm Broke!* by Patricia King will inspire you in any circumstance you will ever face. Learn to turn any situation around by a divine shift from being a victim to a victor by the lessons in this user-friendly book.

JAMES W. GOLL
Encounters Network • Prayer Storm • Compassion Acts
Author of *The Seer, Dream Language, The Lost Art of Intercession, The Coming Israel Awakening,* and many more
www.jamesgoll.com

CONTENTS

FOREWORD

by Heidi Baker

Patricia's book has been a joy for my husband Rolland and me to read. It brings the excitement of supernatural faith for finances into the real and practical world where we all live. It is truly refreshing and satisfying, precisely because it fully acknowledges the warning of Jesus that we cannot serve both God and money. It completely avoids the idea that spirituality is a way to gain wealth. Instead it gloriously underscores the fact that God can and will sustain us in a way that gives us the greatest possible blessing, just as our hearts of faith and love are a blessing to Him. With the writer of Proverbs we ask for neither poverty nor riches, but that perfect provision which keeps us godly and content, rich toward Him. With too much, we forget God; and with too little, we become bitter. He knows how to love us!

Rolland and I laughed, nodded, reminisced and rejoiced over all of Patricia's stories, which so reminded us of our own walk of faith that began when we launched out into the mission field over thirty years ago. Like Patricia, we determined in the Lord that it was possible to believe the Gospel and live out the Sermon on the Mount, trusting our Heavenly Father for everything without anxiety and desperate pleading for help. We have a Perfect Savior, and in Him we can face poverty and disaster anywhere in the world with the Good News that no situation is hopeless. Of course, also like Patricia, our faith was tested beyond anything we could have anticipated.

At our wedding we asked for ticket money, not towels and china sets. After the ceremony we eagerly counted up what we had received, which turned out to be just enough for one-way tickets to Indonesia and about thirty dollars. Two weeks and many miracles later, we charged off to Bali, and for months we existed on almost nothing. We had clear direction about going, so we weren't presumptuous, but we lost a lot of weight. Rolland's wedding ring dropped off his finger, and I had to get him another one when he fattened up later in the States. We survived on noodles given to us by villagers in the jungle, with occasional eggs tossed in. Once in awhile someone took us to dinner. We had no vehicle for years, and when we finally got one, it was a rusted, leaking, roach-infested old station wagon, but it ran, and we were thrilled! We ministered to the poor so we thought it was honorable to be poor, really poor. We didn't eat cheese, take hot baths, or buy nice clothes. When traveling, we lived in garages and on living room floors. Often without basic bus or train money, we walked and waited for rides or outright miraculous provision. Once, when I was pregnant, we slept in a bicycle shed in a rolled-up carpet in freezing weather. But over and over Jesus would provide in completely unexpected ways. Often it wasn't the rich at all who helped us, but the least likely.

Later we gained some faith and began to lead teams on six-month evangelistic trips to Asia, often without knowing from day to day where we were going to stay or how we were going to eat. But we learned to give, freely, wildly and without compulsion. And we have to say here that Patricia is one of the most generous, extravagant givers to the poor and needy we have ever known. We know that if we are stingy, we will really go broke! As time went on, we trusted God for more and more. For awhile we wavered and got into serious credit card debt. But we stopped, drew a line, and knew we could not continue in ministry with that debt. In one day it was totally paid when an old friend tithed the sale of his house to us. And we have never been in debt since.

We enthusiastically endorse Patricia's practical advice. Powerful faith for miraculous provision needs to be married to common sense and prudent planning. Waste and extravagance that is not a real blessing to us are dishonoring to the Gospel. We need to distinguish between knowing what God wants in a given situation and plain foolishness. Patricia is not advocating that we prove our spiritual status with our elevated lifestyles, but rather that we win the respect of onlookers. Diligence, hard work, determination and sacrifice to meet goals are also profitable qualities in the Kingdom as our motives are sanctified by the Holy Spirit. We aim not for immediate, selfish gratification, but to attain the promises of God through faith and patience in a way that most glorifies Him.

Over time we learned to trust God not only for ourselves and our ministry teams, but also for increasing numbers of orphaned and abandoned children in our new mission field of Mozambique, Africa. As our ministry kept expanding to include many bases and communities of faith, we came to be responsible for property, schools, buildings, equipment, teachers, work forces and needs of many kinds. By experience we know that God, who has raised many from the dead in this country, can also bring hope to the poorest of the poor.

Mozambique has been the world's poorest country, but it is climbing steadily and being greatly impacted by revival that is spreading all over the country. Our situation and our lessons of faith have been drastic, but our joy is that as a result of great testing we can confirm with all the more confidence what Patricia has written in this book. We can identify with the principles she has set out, and know that this book will be a powerful tool in the hands of the Holy Spirit to set captives free from negativity and financial hopelessness. But her confidence is not just in impersonal principles and positive thinking, but in a life-giving spiritual romance with God, on whom we can cast all our care.

Over the years we have repeatedly seen tens of thousands, and sometimes hundreds of thousands of dollars come in miraculously at just the right time. We have poured millions into Mozambique, and have learned to feed thousands of children, staff and workers by simple faith in Jesus. But this came only after learning the ways of God through years of trial and discipline. We are still learning, a bit at a time, as we go lower still and put no confidence in the flesh. We have learned enough to know that Patricia is right on track, and we are so pleased to be able to recommend this book to any who are financially stressed. What works in Africa under the worst conditions we have found, and what has worked all through Patricia's life of ministry, will also work for those anywhere who are humble, pure and trusting enough to receive her volume of treasured counsel.

HEIDI G. BAKER, PhD
Pemba, Mozambique
September 2010

Chapter 1

HELP, GOD!
I'M BROKE!

Chapter 1

HELP, GOD! I'M BROKE!

Jane Gressler was a budding free-lance journalist, married for eight years, and a mother of two children, ages 6 and 4. She shared a good life with her husband Don. They purchased a beautiful home that was affordable with their two incomes. Both of them drove high-end luxury vehicles and owned all the bells and whistles that brought them enjoyment in life. Jane hired workers to clean the house, look after the garden, and help her with the children. They had a great deal of debt because they either charged on credit cards or applied for bank loans in order to make their purchases. As a result, they were loaded with monthly payments, but they also had good incomes that could cover these.

Jane was very happy with her marriage, family, and career. One day, however, her world fell apart. She discovered that her husband was having an affair with one of her closest friends. When she confronted them, they admitted that they were in love with each other. Her husband left her for this woman and filed for divorce.

The divorce process was both expensive and emotionally taxing on Jane. There were no actual assets to split since they owed money on everything they owned. Through the divorce settlement she was granted custody of the children and ownership of the house. Her husband agreed to pay $2,000 per month to support their children and $500 per month for spousal support.

The first and second mortgage payments on their 5,000 square foot home, with taxes and insurance, totaled over $4,300 per month. Jane's lease payment on her vehicle was $680 per month and there were four years left on her commitment. She could not get released from her lease without paying an unaffordable penalty.

Although she could not downsize her vehicle, she did decide to sell the house in order to move into more affordable housing. During that time, however, the housing market crashed and Jane was unable to sell her home. In fact, it listed for only $280,000 in the depressed short-sale market, while she still owed over $500,000. A recession had hit and many of her clients dropped their contracts due to cutbacks. Her world was falling apart around her. She was emotionally broken, devastated, and financially BROKE! One day she was living the high life and the next day she could barely afford food for the children. She had lost everything!

Jane spiraled into a deep depression, hidden away in her room most days with the blinds drawn. She lacked motivation to care for her home or herself, but did her best to look after the children. A concerned neighbor checked in on her regularly and invited her to attend a women's Bible study. Jane declined the offer consistently, but the neighbor was persistent. As a result, Jane finally agreed to join her for the group study one morning.

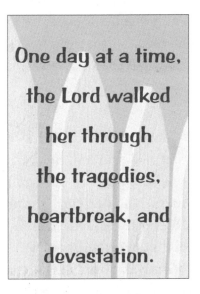

One day at a time, the Lord walked her through the tragedies, heartbreak, and devastation.

That day changed her life. The Lord deeply touched her in that meeting and Jane gave her heart and life to Jesus Christ. Through prayer she gave Christ her devastation and asked for HELP ... and He did!

From that day on, her life progressively transformed into something beautiful. One day at a time, the Lord walked her through the tragedies, heartbreak, and devastation. She did lose her home, but the Lord opened up new doors of opportunity for her – she stepped into her glorious future.

Within two years of the divorce, Jane and her children were established in the blessings of God. She lived a simple yet full life. The Lord granted her one miracle after another. Jane had been shattered in every area of her life. She was both broke and broken, but God restored, healed, and helped her recover all that was important to her. Jane had prayed, *"HELP, GOD – I'M BROKE!"* and, HE DID!

I know of many similar stories. You might not relate to the specifics of Jane's situation, but perhaps you can identify with financial loss, lack, or even overwhelming debt you cannot pay. Maybe you feel like you are spinning your wheels and can't seem to move forward. No matter what your situation is, God is greater! He is powerful and He will help you.Why? Because He loves you and He can!

My Personal Testimony

My husband and I were in our early twenties when we married and had not yet come to know Christ as our personal Savior. We were blessed financially. My husband labored in a lucrative transport industry and I enjoyed a nursing career. We both received comfortable salaries. Through wise financial stewardship we were able to enjoy a wonderful, full life. We always had more than enough and were able to accomplish our financial goals.

When we came to Christ a few years into our marriage, we realized that the blessings we enjoyed were ultimately from Him. They always had been, even before we knew Him. He is the source of all blessing. As new believers, we honored Him with our tithes and offerings – everything increased all the more as a result. We always remembered to praise and thank Him for the goodness shown to us.

Before we were thirty years old, we owned two fully furnished homes and, although the bank held the mortgages, we had no credit card debt, secondary loans, or car payments. We paid cash for everything and delighted in the monthly increase we placed in our savings account.

As we grew in the Lord, our desire to serve Him on the mission field increased. We were very much involved with our local church evangelism outreaches, yet we longed to reach out more to the lost. A young couple in our church went through a YWAM (Youth With A Mission) program and returned with amazing testimonies. We were excited as we heard them share about the miracles the Lord performed on their behalf on a regular basis.

I particularly loved the stories of His miracle provision. They shared how sometimes their team members would be waiting in the airport with neither money nor tickets for the flight to their short-term mission's outreach destination. They waited at the airport in faith, trusting God for supernatural provision. I remember when they testified that a complete stranger approached their friend with a ticket to their exact destination, and then vanished. Perhaps God had sent an angel to them in that situation, or maybe a very sensitive and obedient believer. Another time, they shared how money appeared in the lining of a jacket, meeting their need almost to the penny. Yet another time food was brought to them as they were praising God.

I loved hearing these testimonies. These individuals had no visible means of support and yet the Lord was supplying supernaturally as they served Him in the mission fields of the world. I believed that giving our lives to God for the advancement of His Kingdom was the most awesome way to live, and as a result of their influence we made a decision to attend YWAM's Discipleship Training School in Hawaii in the fall of 1980. In order to take the time off, our employers required that we resign our positions, as they were not able to grant us a leave of absence.

My husband had worked for his employer eleven years and would lose his seniority if he left. I had served in my workplace for four years. We weighed our decision carefully before the Lord, but felt strong confirmation that we were to take the leap of faith and go for it. We resigned our jobs and sold one of our homes to pay off the other. The profit from the house sale gave us the finances to take our entire family to the training school in Hawaii for seven months. We rented our remaining home to a family who had just moved to Canada and needed short-term housing. We planned to use the collected rental income to give us a cushion for the first couple of months after the YWAM training was completed. We were excited to launch into this new faith adventure.

The YWAM training was full of insights and revelation. We learned so many valuable lessons and daily absorbed the testimonies of those who were "living by faith." It was exciting to hear about the miracles of provision God gave to those who trusted Him. We did not actually need miracles at the time as we had our needs met through our savings, but I personally longed to be in a position where I could see the hand of God move in that supernatural way in our personal lives.

Well, that day came! When we returned home to Canada, the recession in the '80s had hit our region hard and my husband was unable to secure employment. He had never been out of work! I had a few on-call shifts at the hospital, but they always conflicted with opportunities to lead outreaches or to share with church groups and Bible studies. I complained in prayer one day, "Lord, You are going to have to coordinate the on-call shifts at the hospital with the evangelism opportunities, because the schedules are not working!"

He responded with a question, "Did I instruct you to go back to work at the hospital?" The inquiry caught me off guard. I believed that my work as a nurse was a vital ministry in itself, as all marketplace involvement is. I responded in thought, "You are not asking me to step out of nursing, are You?" – I loved nursing and I thoroughly enjoyed the medical field. God could not possibly be asking me to step down, I argued with myself, or ... was He?"

After much prayer and wrestling, I received clear confirmation that the Lord was inviting me to step down from my nursing career. He assured me that I would never be sorry. I turned in my resignation when I was completely confident of His leading, even though it did not make sense that I would make this move during the recession when employment was almost nonexistent. Many were losing their jobs. The city we lived in had the highest unemployment rate per capita in North America during that time.

Even with all these considerations, we were convinced we had heard the Lord. He clearly revealed that in this season we would learn to live with no visible means of support. We were to "only" believe. He emphasized that we were not to share our needs with others unless they asked, and we were not to receive from any government institutions like the welfare system. Our trust was to be in Him alone. We wholeheartedly agreed and made the quality decision to move forward. Once we did that, we knew there was no turning back.

Initially, we were actually very excited for the opportunity, as we remembered all the faith-building Bible stories we had studied and the testimonies we heard in YWAM of supernatural provision for those who had needs. Now was our chance. We had a few months of living expenses saved up so it was easy to "believe" in the beginning of this new faith journey, with the backup of our bank account. The savings, however, soon emptied. Then we were face-to-face with our needs.

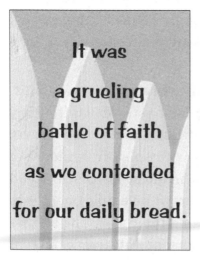

It was a grueling battle of faith as we contended for our daily bread.

In the beginning of our walk of faith, we made a commitment to stand on the Word of God and not compromise what the Lord had revealed and promised. We searched the Scriptures from Genesis through Revelation, embracing the promises and biblical testimonies of provision. We had one path to walk on. That was the path of faith in God's promises of provision. There was no *opt-out* plan available.

We soon discovered there were real demons in the unseen realm named Lack, Poverty, Discouragement, and Fear. I think that every one of these demons in the entire universe came looking for us during this season in our lives! At first we were brave and confident, standing our ground on the promises. But from time to time, fear and discouragement tempted us (well, actually, *many* times ... and it was more like they "gripped" us rather than lightly tempting us, if you know what I mean!).

Many of our friends and relatives questioned our decisions, and some openly judged us. It was not an easy time. We did see some miracle provision once in a while, but most of the time it was a grueling battle of faith as we contended for our daily bread. I wish I could tell you this battle continued for only a few months or even just a year or two, but it actually filled five whole years.

Instead of getting better by the day, it got worse. Many times we questioned ourselves. "Did we make the right choice?" "Should we have ever left our jobs and gone to YWAM?" "Should I go back to my nursing job?" (After the second year of letting my license lapse, even that option was gone.) "Perhaps we should just give in and let everyone know our needs."

We were very diligent in that season and served the Lord every single day and night. My husband is blessed with a true ministry of helps. He loves serving people and helping them solve their problems. He is good at what he does. (Sometimes folks believe that *ministry* refers only to a preacher or a pastor, but the ministry of helps is a valid ministry in the body of Christ and is just as important as other gifts.)

Ron daily went door to door in our community asking folks if he could serve them in any way. Many were poor and discouraged due to the recession, so they couldn't pay anything. He would explain, "You don't have to give me anything. I believe that if I am diligent to serve the Lord, He will take care of my needs." He ministered to many people by cutting their grass, washing their windows, washing down their driveways, and repairing their broken appliances, vehicles, and equipment.

Sometimes people would give him some breakfast muffins, a bag of fruit, or meat from their freezer. Other times they would hand him a little cash, and sometimes they simply shook his hand and thanked him for serving them. Most of the time, he came home with a little something. Our trust was in God and not in what Ron could bring home each day. The Lord also used Ron to pray for people, share the gospel, and give encouragement to all he served.

We were perfectly set up to learn to live by faith with no visible means of support. Every day and every hour we were forced to lean on God. We had no other option. Poverty came knocking at the door of our hearts and minds frequently, but we never allowed it in. We constantly reminded ourselves that the Word of God was true and that God was watching over His Word to perform it (Jeremiah 1:12)! We meditated on the truth and confessed the truth daily. After all, we were the head and not the tail – above and not underneath (Deuteronomy 28:13).

We believed in aligning with the Word regarding Kingdom economic principles. As a result, we never failed to give our tithe (a tenth of our income) to the Lord. In addition, we sowed offerings. Some might think that if you do not have any money to look after your needs, tithing or giving offerings is out of the question. We so believed the Word of God that we never wanted to disobey or compromise in our giving (more on this subject in a later chapter). We also obeyed the principles of diligence, integrity, and wisdom. In no way were we idle during that season, or foolish in our financial decisions.

We daily aligned ourselves with God's Word and His ways, but we did not usually see immediate results. We were being tested, for sure. We fought the good fight of faith every day, and I mean we fought! The Word promised that the pressure we experienced was producing an eternal weight of glory for us (2 Corinthians 4:17). We learned so much.

I admit that I was not *Super-Faith Woman* every moment of this season. No! There were moments when I cried, screamed, and wailed. I was anxious and stressed at times, too, but the Lord was so gracious. Whenever I realized that my thoughts, emotions, and actions were not aligned with the promises of God, I confessed to the Lord and asked Him to forgive me. He did. I knew that I had a clean slate to move forward every time I humbled myself in His presence.

When God looks back upon my journey, He sees only a perfect walk, because all the imperfections are washed away in Christ. I've been reviewing my failures for you at this time to help and encourage you. First John 1:9 says, "If we confess our sins, He is faithful and righteous to forgive us our sins and to cleanse us from all unrighteousness." When God forgives and cleanses, there is nothing left. God is so good!!!

We walked through the five-year testing period learning to live with no visible means of support. Throughout this book I will share many testimonies of God's miracle provision that was granted to us during that time. We truly did become acquainted with the God of Supernatural Provision. During the times when there was NO food in the cupboards, NO gas in the vehicle, NO money in the bank, God came through. According to everything in the natural, we were BROKE – and yet we weren't.

We learned that God was more than enough for us – each and every moment of every day. He was and continues to be our fullness, our abundance. During that period we did not understand that God was preparing us for a global, apostolic, prophetic ministry that would impact nations. We had no idea that we would need to believe for millions of dollars on a regular basis in order to reach the masses with the Word,

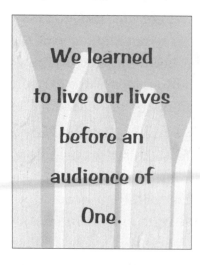

We learned to live our lives before an audience of One.

love of God, and care for the poor and the afflicted. Although we did not allow poverty into our life, we were close enough to it that we carry a deep empathy this day for the poor. We love the poor!

Like mighty King David who learned about God's power and ways as he cared for sheep out in the field, the Lord taught us powerful lessons in hiddenness and aloneness. Like with John the Baptist, God met us in the back side of the wilderness and revealed His truth and ways. At times it did feel like we were merely a small, faint voice proclaiming God's truth – in His presence alone.

As difficult as it was, I wouldn't trade that season for anything. We became very aware of our complete, uncompromising commitment to the Lord. That season introduced us to depths of God's heart that we would never have known otherwise. We learned to live our lives before an audience of One.

God is All We Need

I once heard a story about a faithful missionary who was serving the Lord in an African nation devastated by severe famine. When food portions and supplies arrived from overseas, they quickly trumpeted the news to the hungry villagers within a fifty-mile radius. The organization they served would set up a large tent and organize the distribution of the food rations in the midst of a large plain while the hungry came from the villages. One day, after all the people were fed and the workers had cleaned up the tent, the missionary looked toward the horizon and saw a frail, older gentleman shuffling along the path toward the tent. She quickly sent a driver to get him. On his arrival, she met him, helped him out of the Jeep, and seated him on a bench. He sat there quietly with parched lips and an empty cup in hand.

Looking into his expectant eyes, she explained to him with remorse, "Sir, we have no more food. We gave everything we had away already. There is nothing left." He quietly looked down at his empty cup for a moment and then lifted his head, gazing into her eyes. "That's OK," he answered. "You never know that Jesus is all you need until Jesus is all you have."

35

That story left a powerful imprint on my heart. Oh how true! He is all we need. Sometimes when we come to the end of ourselves, when we are personally bankrupt, we encounter and experience this wonderful reality.

Jesus taught, "Blessed are the poor in spirit, for theirs is the kingdom of heaven" (Matthew 5:3). When we understand our total and complete dependency upon Him, then we shall experience the power and the glory of the Kingdom of God. We shall see His intervention. We shall see His grace. He is more precious than anything money can buy!

Whatever you are facing right now, God is greater. He loves you so deeply and desires to bring you through to a place of deep blessing and increase in every good thing. His desire is for you to experience heaven on earth.

You Were Created for Blessing!

The word *blessing* means to have goodness bestowed upon you – and that includes abundant provision. You desire the goodness and abundant provision of God to manifest in your life because you were created for it. It feels good and it feels right when you are blessed, because it is God's plan. After God created mankind, He made a decree that involved fruitfulness and increase, not lack and poverty: "God blessed them; and God said to them, 'Be fruitful and multiply' " (Genesis 1:28).

One of the definitions of *bless* in the Merriam-Webster On-line Dictionary is, "to confer prosperity or happiness upon."

In Deuteronomy 28:2, we discover a promise that is so amazing, and it belongs to anyone who qualifies. It says, "*All these blessings will come upon you and overtake you."* The blessings listed in the next twelve verses mainly relate to provisional blessings. What a great picture: provisional blessings coming upon you and overtaking you.

The scenario that this Scripture reminds me of is that of a football game, when a player has been aggressively tackled from behind and brought down. His opponent came upon him and overtook him. Imagine what it would be like if God's abundant provision came upon you in that way. This does not depend on your current financial status. You might think, "How can that possibly happen to me? I am in debt up to my eyeballs. I am broke!"

Deuteronomy 28:1 gives the terms of qualification and the instruction for posturing yourself to receive the blessings: "**If you will diligently obey all the commandments**" (emphasis mine). We cannot fulfill all the commandments of God in our own strength, but Jesus fulfilled all righteousness for you two thousand years ago. He opened the way for you to live in all the promises, all the time. All the blessings listed in Deuteronomy 28:1-14, and in the rest of the Bible, are yours – not because you obeyed all the commandments, but because He did. The blessings of abundant provision are not yours because you are worthy, but because He is. He fulfilled the requirements and gave you the blessings – blessings that will come upon you and overtake you on a perpetual basis. As you enjoy the fullness of Christ's life and righteousness within you, the values of the Kingdom will manifest in your life as in His. To disobey the Word and wisdom of God will bring disaster to your life, but to allow His life to live through you will bring life, peace, and prosperity. God's Word has clear instruction and wisdom for you regarding your financial prosperity. When you follow Him and His ways, you will find blessings coming upon you and overtaking you.

When my grandson was a baby, I played a game with him. I crawled on the floor behind him and said, "Grandma's going

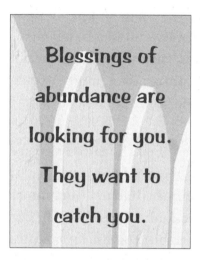

Blessings of abundance are looking for you. They want to catch you.

to get you." He actually wanted me to get him. He would attempt to crawl away from me so that I could catch him. That was the fun part. He would laugh and then attempt to crawl away again, looking back to see if I was going to come and catch him up into my arms and kiss him all over. Of course I got him every time. I came up from behind and overtook him with love hugs and kisses. At five years of age, he still enjoyed the *Grandma's-going-to-get-you* game, and his little sisters have picked up on it really well, too. This is a great picture of how blessings can come upon you and overtake you. Blessings of abundance are looking for you. They want to catch you. They want to "get you." And of course, you want them to. Right?

All the Blessings Are Yours

Ephesians 1:3 says, "Blessed be the God and Father of our Lord Jesus Christ, who has blessed us with every spiritual blessing in the heavenly places in Christ." Through the finished work of the cross you have been blessed with every spiritual blessing. Jesus explained to us that the glory the Father gave Him, He has freely given to us (John 17:22). The word *glory (doxa)* in that context includes all the blessings of who God is and what He has. You are called to live in the abundance of these blessings. The Scripture calls them "spiritual blessings in Christ." They are called *spiritual* because they are in the unseen or spiritual dimension before they manifest in the natural. They are secured for you in the heavenly places in Christ where He is seated at the right hand of the Father. They are therefore safe from the influence of the demonic because they are in Christ. In another chapter I will teach you how to exercise your faith in order to download all these blessings into your "now."

You Have Everything You Need Right Now

You do not need to wait until the chariots come to take you away to "the sweet by and by" to live a life of blessing. This is your portion NOW due to Christ's finished work of the cross. Peter wrote,

> His divine power has granted to us everything pertaining to life and godliness, through the true knowledge of Him who called us by His own glory and excellence. For by these He has granted to us His precious and magnificent promises, so that by them you may become partakers of the divine nature, having escaped the corruption that is in the world by lust. —2 Peter 1:3-4

Your Financial Situation Can Change, and It Will!

I know it might be difficult to imagine your current financial situation changing right now, but if you put your trust in Christ, it will! Your complete breakthrough is only one miracle away. That's right! Most of the time when we face difficulties, all we need is one miracle.

Some people say, "Oh, I could pay off all my debts and live an abundant life if I could just win the lottery." Studies implemented to follow up on winners of lotteries reveal that within a short time, the individuals are right back where they started. They had an intervention that set them free momentarily but they never changed their thinking and their way of doing things.

Jesus wants to intervene for you, and He will. But He also wants you to **remain and continually abide** in the blessing of abundance. He does not just want to give you a quick fix, but a permanent flow of "more than enough"! A miracle can deliver you in a moment from the pressures you face, but good mentorship by the Spirit of God will keep you free for a lifetime if you yield to His ways.

I believe you will experience financial freedom. I have prayed for everyone who reads this book to be visited by God's wisdom and revelation that grants the keys to long-term financial breakthrough and blessing. There is nothing impossible for God. He loves you so deeply and is eternally committed to your prosperity. Believe that! Yield to Him! He is all you need right now. If you could have overcome your situation with your own resources and strength, you would not have bought this book. Your past self-efforts to deliver yourself from your financial bondage more than likely catapulted you into the situation you are in now.

You need His help and He is committed to giving it to you! An intervention is on its way. Jesus said, "The thief comes only to steal and kill and destroy; I came that they may have life, and have it abundantly" (John 10:10). Jesus also left a Helper with you. He is Holy Spirit. You cannot see Him with your visible eyes, but He is with you at all times to offer you help, counsel, and support while you are on the earth (see John 14:16-17, 26; 16:13-15).

If you are willing to completely surrender to Jesus and allow Holy Spirit to lead you into established victory, He will. The Holy Spirit is also offering you a lifetime mentorship on living in abundance and blessing all your days.

Come to Jesus

If you have not yet come to know Jesus as your personal Savior, or if you have received Him into your heart as a Savior but not as true Lord (Owner) and King (Ruler) of your life, then pray this prayer and begin a brand new life today:

Lord Jesus,

I believe that You are Savior, Lord, and King. I admit that I need your help, as I have come to the end of myself. I choose to give You my life completely. Forgive me of my sins and cleanse me from all unrighteousness. Come into my heart and take the reins.

Have mercy on me and grant me miracle intervention in the situation I am in currently. I believe You are the Restorer of all things. Teach me Your ways, that I might walk in Your paths all the days of my life.

Thank You for Your kindness, Jesus.

AMEN.

Chapter 2

HELP, GOD!

I NEED A MIRACLE!

Chapter 2

HELP, GOD! I NEED A MIRACLE!

There are two realms that surround our lives: the natural realm (the visible realm) and the supernatural realm (the invisible realm). Miracles manifest in your life when the power of God in the supernatural realm enters the natural realm. Imagine for a moment the miracle power of God entering into your bank account and filling it to overflowing. That is a miracle! Imagine the bank calling you on the phone informing you that your debt is paid in full, but they cannot give you an explanation for it. You might think that sounds far out, but I have witnessed such things. Nothing is impossible with God.

45

All you possibly require at this moment is one injection of a miracle into your need. Nothing is too difficult for God, but we often get overwhelmed when we look at our life circumstances and forget how easy even the most difficult situation is for Him.

Banking in the Glory

In Philippians 4:19 we are promised that God will meet all our needs according to His riches in glory in Christ Jesus. That means if you have a need right now, God has it already met. Think of it as a heavenly bank account that is never empty. As a child of God you can make withdrawals on that account.

Katie Souza, a friend of mine, teaches a course called Banking in the Glory. Her ministry, Expected End Ministries, had accrued $21,000 dollars in credit card debt. The interest grew rapidly each month. Because of this, her whole team decided to go on a 21-day fast.

As she was fasting for breakthrough, the Lord gave her understanding about His creative power in the glory cloud. She studied the Scriptures and decided to put her faith to work. She obeyed what the Scriptures revealed to her. At that time they only had $3,000 dollars to pay on $21,000 dollars of credit card bills. She positioned herself before God to wait for His glory presence and pressed in with the power of thanksgiving to open the gates of heaven.

She then used her praise to enter the courts of His presence where His glory and creative power resides. In that posture, by faith, she contended for her miracle as she continued to keep her mind and heart focused in worship. No matter how many times she got distracted, she kept bringing her focus back to the Lord. She continued to press in until a shift in the atmosphere was experienced around her and inside of her. She then spoke into the glory presence even as God did in the very beginning of time, when He declared, "Let there be light," and there was light. She lifted up her $3,000 into the glory presence and in Jesus' name commanded it to be blessed and to prosper.

Following this prayer time in the glory, Katie divided the $3,000 and made payments on the credit cards. After the 21-day fast ended, she received an anonymous gift of $21,000 dollars for her ministry! She was able to pay off the entire credit card debt.

She now constantly relies on the creative power of the Lord's glory whenever she needs a financial miracle. Within one year following this revelation and encounter, her ministry received over a million dollars in miracles. God truly will meet all your needs according to His riches in glory by Christ Jesus! Banking in the glory is for real!

Daily Miracles

Position yourself for a miracle. Get excited! Allow your expectancy to grow. Do not be overwhelmed with what you are facing right now, but look to God and His greatness. Jesus said to pray in this way, "Give us this day our daily bread" (Matthew 6:11). Don't be anxious about tomorrow; believe for His grace today. Take one day at a time. God will open the heavens over you and pour out a blessing that will meet your need today.

Israel saw the miracle provision of God every day as they journeyed through the wilderness. They had lived in bondage for 400 years and served under cruel taskmasters in Egypt. God delivered them out of Egypt by His mighty hand and promised them their own land – a land flowing with milk and honey where they would eat food without scarcity and enjoy abundance in all things. They were happy with the promise, though they lost sight of it when they walked through the desert with no visible means of support.

Position yourself for a miracle. Get excited! Allow your expectancy to grow.

There was no food or water anywhere, but this was not a problem for God. He opened the heavens and rained down manna, a bread-like substance, so that every individual could eat as much as they wanted every day. There was no water, but God provided water for them from a rock. Who has ever heard of a rock pouring out water for over a million people every day? You do not need to fear, even if you can't see any hope of provision. God can easily open the heavens and bring you what you need from an unexpected source. He wants to.

$20 bills and cup hooks

When our family was going through our season of learning to live by faith with no visible means of support, I felt the unction of the Spirit to attend a prayer gathering for the First

Nations people in Ottawa, Canada. My husband said that he would care for our home and family if I went, but we had no money for the ticket and the trip. It required God's provision. By faith I contacted a travel agent and she quoted me the sale price of $189 for the airfare. There was a deadline for the purchase of the ticket at that price. We prayed in faith, but no funding came in.

The night before the last day of the sale, I had a dream. In the dream, the hand of God put a stack of $20 bills in my hand. He then laid His other hand on the stack and said, "Go buy your ticket!" I told my husband the dream before he left for the day, and then I proceeded to prepare my sons for school. I opened the dish cupboard and set the table for breakfast. I did not notice anything unusual in the cupboard. After breakfast we washed the dishes, put them away, and left the house for school. I was the last one out, so I locked the door behind me.

After dropping the boys off at school, I went to visit a friend who was in crisis and had requested some prayer support. I ministered to her and then excused myself to attend a scheduled prayer meeting that I was now late for. On my way out the door she said, "Wait for just a moment, please." She ran back into the house and returned with some money. She said, "The Lord just told me to give you this." She handed me five $20 bills totaling $100. I was blown away!

I drove to the prayer meeting and enjoyed interceding for our city for an hour or two with some friends. Then I quietly left the meeting to pick up my sons for lunch. I was getting into my car when suddenly a woman ran out after me and said, "Patricia, the Lord just told me to give you this." She put a $20 bill in my hand. I was once again elated and excited about the delivery of the $20 bills. I still had a number of hours left to purchase my ticket. Expectancy arose in my heart. "How was God going to complete this?" I wondered.

After thanking her, I collected the boys from school, put the key in our front door and opened it. The three of us walked in and I quickly went to the cupboard to get the dishes for lunch. Upon opening the cupboard door, I noticed $20 bills hanging on cup hooks – five $20 bills. With the other $20 bills I had received earlier, I now had a total of $220. This was more than what I needed. God is the God of more than enough! How did the $20 bills get there? Did an angel bring them? Did God materialize them? I know for sure that I was the last one to go out the door and I had locked it. There were no $20 bills there before I left. It had to be a miracle.

After lunch I drove the boys back to school and headed straight to the travel agent. She booked my flight and said, "That will be $218, please." I questioned, "But I thought the seat sale was $189?" She replied, "The rest is taxes and airport improvement fees." God knew what I needed even though I didn't. He is so wonderful!

Creative Miracles

In Genesis 1, we discover that God created something out of nothing. There was no light in the earth before God said, "Let there be light." There were no plants in the earth until God said, "Let the earth sprout vegetation, plants yielding seed, and fruit trees on the earth bearing fruit after their kind with seed in them." God can grant you a creative miracle. You might think, "There is nothing in my hand to work with. My bank account is empty. My bills are not paid."

Don't try to figure out how God is going to do it. He can create something out of nothing. Ponder that for a few minutes. Imagine what it would be like in your situation if God were to create a full bank account for you or fill your cupboards with food or your closet with clothes. Imagine the possibility of waking up one morning and finding a car in your garage that you never purchased, but the registration has your name on it. He can create things that are not there.

Cars need gas – or do they?

In our season of testing, I was the not-so-proud owner of a small car that was rusted, had a hole in the floor, and needed ropes to tie the doors shut. In the winter, the heater didn't function so I bundled up in a warm moth-eaten fur coat that I had purchased at the thrift shop for $15. My legs were kept warm by a pair of boots that were missing a chunk of leather on the top of the left boot (due to our dog chewing it off one day). The one benefit was that this car was great on gas consumption and therefore cost us very little to operate.

One night I completed ministry at a meeting in Vancouver, approximately 50 miles from our home, and noticed there was no gas in the tank. It registered below empty! Initially, I panicked. "What am I going to do?" I went into prayer and felt the Lord say, "Drive home." I was a bit apprehensive since there were desolate patches along the highway and I did not want to run out of fuel late at night in these isolated areas. Again, I heard the still small voice say, "Drive home." So, I did! I kept my eyes fixed on the gas gauge and to my amazement it started to climb. The longer I drove, the more it climbed. By the time I arrived home, I had almost a full tank of gas. This was a creative miracle – God created gas in the tank.

Your words create miracles

Your words are very powerful. James teaches this about the power of the tongue: "The tongue is a fire ... and sets on fire the course of our life" (James 3:6). Your God-inspired spoken words, declared in faith, can create miracles.

My bookkeeper sends me monthly financial reports for our ministries and businesses. One month I noticed that the balance on one of our accounts was extremely low. I sought the Lord and He gave me some wise instruction to obey. In addition I felt led to make God-inspired spoken decrees over the account.

> If I am to have faith for multiplication, then I must contend for a double portion at least.

Try this sometime: print out your bank statement and cross out the old balance. Then replace the actual balance with the balance you desire. By faith, call that balance in. Speak to the account. Say, "Account, be filled in Jesus' name to this amount. Money, come!" Put your revised bank statement in your journal. Every time you look at it, thank the Lord for a creative miracle that is filling the account. You might think this sounds silly, but I have found this act of faith to create miraculous results.

Deuteronomy 8:18 says, "But you shall remember the Lord your God, **for it is He who is giving you power to make wealth,** that He may confirm His covenant" (emphasis mine). You have been given the power to create wealth according to God's covenant with Abraham. This covenant is now yours in Christ. Use that creative power to release miracles into your financial situation today.

Miracles of Multiplication

When God blessed mankind, He said, "Be fruitful and MULTIPLY." One day, while desiring increase for one of our financial goals, I asked the Lord to give me some added provision. I believed Him for the next level, which was about 15 percent more than what we were receiving. He lovingly rebuked me and emphasized, "I did not say to be fruitful and **add.**" I said, "Be fruitful and **multiply!**" I realized at that moment that the lowest factor for multiplication is double, so if I am to have faith for multiplication, then I must contend for a double portion at least.

The widow's miracle

In 1 Kings 17:9-16 we find Elijah in the midst of a terrible famine. He was instructed to go to the city of Zarephath where God had commanded a widow to provide for him. When he entered the city, he asked a widow to get him some water and to bring him a little bread. She responded, "As the Lord your God lives, I have no bread, only a handful of flour in the bowl and a little oil in the jar; and behold, I am gathering a few sticks that I may go in and prepare for me and my son, that we may eat it and die." In other words, she was saying, "I'm broke and I have nothing to give to you!"

Your "little" is often a catalyst for a miracle!

When we are in need, we often do not see what we have. Our "little" does not seem like anything at all, but as we are about to discover, your little is often the catalyst for a miracle! Elijah instructed the widow to take the little flour and oil she had left and make him a cake. He asked her to do this first so that she could experience a miracle.

The prophet Elijah represents the Word of God in Scripture, so it would be like us giving first to Jesus, who is the Word that became flesh. After she made him a cake, he instructed her to make one for herself and her son. This is interesting because she only had enough to make a cake for herself and her son in the beginning. She has used what she had for Elijah's cake, and yet he now instructs her to make one for her and her son. He promised that if she would step out in obedience to fulfill this word, her flour and oil would not be exhausted for the entire famine.

She followed through, making Elijah a little cake of bread and giving it to him. This was the beginning of her miracle of multiplication. What you give into the hands of Jesus becomes the substance for your miracle. After she fed Elijah, she went back to her flour and oil and discovered that there was enough to make another one for herself and her son. Every time she made a cake of bread, the flour and oil increased. She had enough food for the entire famine. She had stepped into living in the realm of the miraculous in a time where there was hardship all around her. She was living in the miracle zone in the midst of famine.

The secret to this continuous flow in the miraculous was that she used the little she had to be the catalyst. What is in your hand? What do you have? Your little can be the beginning of your miracle.

How did the miracle of the 5,000 work?

In Mark 6:33-44, we read about the miracle of Jesus and His disciples feeding the 5,000. There are some important insights to note in this miracle.

The disciples came to Jesus with a plan. They were in a region where there was no food and the large crowd was going to need some. They made a suggestion to Jesus that He send the crowd away to buy themselves some food. It was a great idea and somewhat thoughtful, but it was not God's idea. Jesus wanted to teach them how to work provisional miracles of multiplication. To feed 5,000 with nothing would definitely take a miracle. Jesus said, "You give them something to eat!"

Their response was probably the same as what you and I would say. "Oh Lord, we can't feed them. We don't have the money to feed that many people!" Jesus, however, was insistent! Let's look at some lessons that we can learn from the working of this miracle.

Lesson One: Do Not Look at Your Lack, Look at What You Have.

In verse 38, Jesus gives us our first important insight. He said to His disciples: "How many loaves do you have? **Go look!**" Just prior to this they had been looking at their lack,

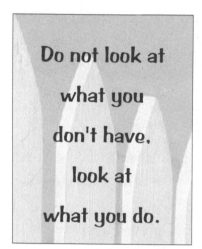

Do not look at what you don't have, look at what you do.

but now He was calling them to look at their potential. They had to go look in order to find what was available. Sometimes we sit around waiting for a miracle to fall out of the sky, but Jesus wants us to be diligent with what we have and with what we can do. What do you have?

When they went and looked, they brought back five loaves and two fish. These loaves were probably not large bread loaves but rather lunch-sized buns. But even at best, no matter how long those loaves were, they were not enough to feed a multitude – or were they?

Your substance for a miracle is probably right in sight even though it might look inadequate and insignificant to you. Do not look at what you don't have, look at what you do.

Lesson Two: Prepare For Your Miracle.

Jesus knew that a miracle would take place, so He prepared. In verses 39 and 40, He organized the multitude by having them all sit on the grass in groups of hundreds and fifties.

Dr. David Yonggi Cho of Seoul, Korea, is the founder of one of the largest churches in the world. When his congregation consisted of only 20 members, he received a revelation from the Lord regarding the faith dimension of the Kingdom of God. His desire was to see multiplication of his church and as his first leap of faith, he believed God for 100 members. This was a 500 percent increase. He prepared by having his deacons set the church up with 100 chairs for the morning service. They did so with reluctance. That morning, the regular number of attendees came, but Cho preached as though there were a hundred. Eventually all those seats were filled. Then he believed for 500, and eventually millions. He did not wait until he received the 100 in order to prepare. He prepared for the miracle of multiplication before it manifested.

Lesson Three: Look to Heaven.

In verse 41, we find Jesus taking the loaves and fishes and, looking up into heaven, He blessed them. Jesus was not looking at His circumstances in the earth. He was looking to the open gates of God's blessings in heaven. He was looking for His miracle.

In Colossians 3:1-2, we are taught to set our minds on the things above where Christ is seated, and not to focus on things in the earth. The heavenly realm is the miracle realm. Look for your miracle. Look to the open portals of glory that Christ opened for you through His finished work on the cross. Look to God's unfailing promises.

As Jesus was looking into heaven and engaging in that realm, He blessed what was in His hand. When you lift what

57

you have into the heavenly dimension and bless it, the earthly offering is thus submitted to the blessing of the glory realm. You are, in this way, invoking a heavenly blessing into earthly substance, making it subject to the law of the Spirit of Life in Christ Jesus while it is in the earth.

After Jesus blessed what was in His hands, the loaves and fishes multiplied according to divine environment and not earthly restriction.

Lesson Four: Keep Giving.

"He ... broke the loaves and He **kept giving** them to the disciples to set before them; and He divided up the two fish among them all" (Mark 6:41 emphasis mine).

Jesus took what appeared small and divided it up amongst his 12 disciples. Sometimes we wait for God to dump a big load of blessing on us before we act on our miracle. I have heard some individuals say to me, "If God gives me a financial miracle, I will bless your ministry with a large sum of money." I know they are probably sincere, but I seldom expect what they say to be realized. The way increase and enlargement comes is to be faithful with the little. Miracles of financial multiplication come through giving the little that is in your hand and then you keep giving as more comes in.

The disciples didn't wait for truckloads of bread and fish to come in before they stepped into the miracle. They received a piece of bread from the hand of Jesus (which couldn't have been very much in the natural – 5 loaves divided into 12 does not give much bread for each disciple to distribute). Jesus kept giving to them. The more He broke the bread and gave it away, the more it was increased in His hand. The more the disciples gave, the more it increased back into their hands. The same happened with the fish.

The increase was so great that after they gave and gave and gave and gave, everyone had as much as they wanted, and there were 12 full baskets left over. They had more than what they began with after it was distributed. Imagine 5,000 hungry men eating as much as they wanted in order to get filled (and that's not to mention their wives and children). How many truckloads would that be? And yet, you did not see one truck. Sometimes you cannot even see the miracle – only the effects of it. Miracles are not always spectacular, but they are always supernatural.

Chicken, chicken, chicken

One Sunday afternoon when our sons were young, Ron had left me at home to cook our chicken dinner while he took the boys skating at a local lake near our home. I made enough dinner for our family of four and was hoping to have some chicken left over to make Ron his sandwiches for work the next day.

This happened back in the days when there were no cell phones, so there was no way for Ron to warn me that he was bringing guests home for dinner. He had met some family and friends while skating and joyfully walked through the door with company for dinner – 19 people total, including our family. I thought I would faint!

All of a sudden that nice chicken I was cooking for the family looked mighty small. I had been studying the story of Jesus feeding the 5,000 just that morning, and a nervous expectation started to arise within me. I needed a miracle right away, so perhaps I would receive one.

Ron brought a large piece of plywood to put on our table. We covered it with a large sheet and set the table for our guests. I added a few more potatoes and vegetables to the pot, but what was I going to do about that chicken? Our only hope was a miracle. I carved the chicken onto a platter, whispering a prayer over every slice of that little bird, "Multiplication! Multiplication!" When I looked at the platter of chicken, I thought, "If everyone takes a small portion, this might work." I prayed for God to make everyone sensitive to the needs of the others.

At the table we started passing the bowls of food around. I passed the platter of chicken to the first guest, but he was not sensitive at all. Oh no! He took a large portion of chicken, enough for two or three people, I thought. I panicked inside, wondering how things would stretch with this type of behavior, but I said nothing. I watched the next guest serve himself a portion. He did the same thing as the first. The third and fourth person also took super-sized portions. I was so stressed – until I looked at the platter.

Were my eyes deceiving me? There seemed to be heaps of chicken remaining, even though four people had already taken large portions. The platter went all around the table. I was the last, and there was still a full platter of chicken! Hey, I also went for the super-sized portion. Why not?

A miracle was taking place right before our eyes. What made it more of a miracle is that some of the guests enjoyed second and third portions and there was still a full platter left. We ate chicken for the next three days. We had chicken sandwiches, chicken soup, chicken casseroles – Chicken! Chicken! Chicken!

Multiplication of fish

In our five-year season of testing, we had very little food or money to buy it. A friend of ours had gone trout fishing, and he gave us two fish from his catch. Once the heads were removed, each fish was about six inches long. I mention this so you will know how small they were. If I cut each one in half, there was just enough to feed our family of four, one small meal.

At this time, our neighbor, who was a widow raising her two children alone, was going through some difficulties. I had been praying for her and wished I could reach out to her. I wanted to invite her for dinner, but I looked at the two small fish I had thawing on the counter and knew that it would not be enough for all of us. However, faith rose in my heart and I gave her a call.

After she accepted the invitation, I was contemplating what I could do with these two little fish to make them stretch – perhaps a rice and fish casserole. I went to the counter to begin my dinner preparations, and when I looked I saw not only my two small fish but a third larger one also. It simply appeared!

What a wonderful time we had together over dinner that night. I shared with her and her children concerning the miracle and it gave her faith to press in for her needs, too.

Jesus is the same, yesterday, today, and forever. He multiplied fish on the shores of Galilee two thousand years ago and He continues to multiply fish today.

Multiplication of "pocket money"

A friend of mine, Dawn Eaves, founder of the Prayer Company, had been on a journey of living with no visible means of support. She was a very faithful Kingdom woman, serving the Lord with a pure heart. She was learning to trust the Lord for her daily bread. Every time she saw one commitment fulfilled,

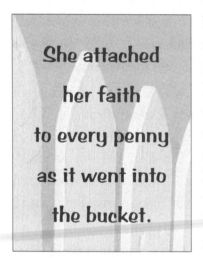

She attached her faith to every penny as it went into the bucket.

then the Lord would call her to believe for a larger challenge. She still struggled with fear and apprehension. By the time she paid her tithe, taxes, rent, and a few other bills, she was broke again and often dipped into her overdraft account. She would hear the Lord speak to her heart through various teachings, "If what you have does not meet the need, it is seed." That began to ruminate within her spirit. She kept asking, "What does that look like in the natural?" She wondered how she could sow into something else when she couldn't even make her own car payment, put food on her table, or gas in her car.

When she attended Christian conferences, she sometimes walked through the parking lots looking for pennies or change that had been dropped or thrown out, just so she could put something in the offering as it went by. She attached her faith to every penny as it went into the bucket. Many times she would sit there and cry as she watched everyone else sow — she wanted her own breakthrough so much. She wanted God to make the promise of multiplication real to her. She wanted to know in the deepest part of her being that God alone was her provision.

At a conference called Kingdom Wealth, she was determined to receive an encounter from the Lord that would answer that very prayer. She had $9 to sow for that entire conference, so she made sure that she sowed some of it in every offering. During one session, she felt a level of faith fill the room, which was a new experience for her at that time. Supernatural and spontaneous giving began to break out. She was down to her last dollar. As she dropped it in the bucket, she began to cry because it was the last one she had. As she was walking back to her chair, she put her hand in her pocket and pulled out a $5 bill that had definitely not been there previously. She ran forward to sow it. When she returned to her seat, she found more. She ran forward and sowed it, and again when she returned there was more. She was finding money in her purse, in her Bible, on the floor under her seat, and in her notebook. It was showing up everywhere.

Money began showing up supernaturally throughout the room, and people started to spontaneously give to one another. That continued throughout the weekend, and by the time the conference was over, she had received supernaturally and sown right back into the glory around $700-

$800 – all from a $9 start. Personal financial breakthrough started manifesting in her life in greater measure than ever before.

The Power of Agreement

Jesus taught that if two or three agree on something in prayer, they will receive it (see Matthew 18:19).

To walk in this promise, first agree with the Word of God concerning your need or desire. Then find another person of unwavering faith who will agree with you. This is very powerful in the Spirit.

Sometimes in a corporate meeting, a word of knowledge or prophecy will come forth indicating the will of God. If you come into agreement with the will of God as it is proclaimed, you can experience the miracle realm.

Provision of houses

In 2008, my friends Georgian and Winnie Banov hosted a conference in Maryland. During a time of prayer, a woman at the altar responded to a word of knowledge revealing that the Lord wanted to give her a house. One hour and fifteen minutes after she sat back down, someone called her on her cell phone and said, "I'm giving you a house." She lifted her cell phone up in the air and started dancing right there at her seat. The conference session was ending and she skipped her way to the front and told everyone the amazing report. They greatly rejoiced over the goodness of God shown her.

A year later, Georgian was led to release that same prayer for new houses during his 2009 conference in San Jose. During the prayer time, a mother stood up in proxy for her daughter who needed a house but had been disqualified by the bankers for weeks. She stood in agreement that her daughter was going to be able to get a house. This prayer of agreement took place during the offering. Later during the altar call and prayer for the sick, that sweet little mama came to the front of the sanctuary literally shaking. She held out her cell phone showing Georgian her text that said, "Mom, I've just been approved for a house!"

A Miracle for You

So, you need a miracle? God has one for you! Believe.

Chapter 3

OH, NO, I'M
IN TROUBLE!

(GOD'S FINANCIAL RESTORATION PLAN)

Chapter 3

OH, NO, I'M IN TROUBLE!

I was waiting for a plane one morning in Phoenix and I noticed the woman beside me. She looked very tired, broken, and distressed. We started up a conversation and immediately she desperately shared her story with me. She was a registered nurse by profession and had traveled to Las Vegas for a few days of vacation. While there, she gambled away everything she owned – EVERYTHING! She was on her way home to face the music, completely broke and completely broken. Now, that is trouble!

I have met many folks who've found themselves in a financial crisis without the answers to escape their situation. They feel imprisoned, hopeless, and sometimes even suicidal. When economic markets crash and individuals lose all their assets, it is reported that numbers of individuals take their lives. The hopelessness and despair is too much for them to bear.

You could be in a situation right now where things look impossible for you. It might not be as dramatic as the story I just shared, but even small situations warrant the loving and merciful intervention of the Lord. I want to help you come into hope and victory no matter how small or how enormous your challenge is. Remember that the Lord is greater than anything you are facing right now.

Jesus taught that "the thief [referring to the devil] comes only to steal" (John 10:10). Proverbs 6:31 teaches that if we catch a thief in the act, he must repay sevenfold what he stole AND we get to plunder his house. I have often declared into the spirit realm when the enemy is harassing me, "Devil, in the name of Jesus, you will be sorry you ever tried!"

You might have just now come to the awareness that you have been robbed of wisdom, finances, and peace. Let the light go on inside you. This awareness means that you have caught the thief in the act! Demand the sevenfold return and plunder the enemy's house. I always let the enemy know he is messing with the wrong person because I have a covenant with God! My God can get me out of any hard place, out of any mess, and He can even clean up any mistake I might have made. You are in good hands when you know the Lord!

Jesus taught us to pray in Matthew 6:12, "Forgive us our debts." What is a debt? Webster's Dictionary states that it is "something owed; the state of owing." The word *debt* in Matthew

6:12 refers to sin and trespass, but it can also be applied to the principle of financial indebtedness. It is possible to live free from debt. We live in a society where credit purchases are encouraged and therefore many people live beyond their means. We are taught to buy, buy, and buy some more, even if we do not have the money to cover it. We sometimes think, "Well, I can afford the payment, so I can have what I want right now." The problem is that those minimum payments add up and usually only cover the interest.

Before long, that new dress you put on your credit card doesn't fulfill you the same as it did the first time you wore it, yet you are still paying on it. The car with three more years of payments now needs new tires, a tune up, and insurance, but you are maxed out with your payments and can't maintain it. The $100 steak dinner that tasted so good has come and gone and you are still hungry, but the credit card debt is a constant reminder of what once was.

We must learn restraint and wisdom in our spending. We need to live within our means. So many are shipwrecked because they wanted what they couldn't afford, and bought it anyway. A simple life can be very fulfilling. When Ron and I lived in leanness for five years, we never went into debt. If we didn't have the money, we didn't spend it. We found fulfilling ways to enjoy life. Instead of going to a movie theatre, we went for a nice walk with the kids in the park. Rather than go out to a restaurant for a meal, we made a tasty pot of soup at home and cooked up some popcorn while we played a board game. We created a quality life that was within our means. If you have money, you can spend it, but if you don't, you shouldn't.

Count the Cost

Sometimes we get into a tight place because of a blind side. A young couple wanted a second vehicle. They went to the car lot and found a beautiful vehicle that was a little beyond their price range, but when they crunched the numbers, they thought they could still make it work. They signed for the car and the payment, but failed to work into their monthly budget the insurance, gas, and maintenance costs of the new vehicle. The extra payment was a huge strain on them, but even worse were all the added costs. They had failed to look at the whole picture of their purchase.

A large commercial lot became available for sale. It had amazing potential for us as a ministry. When I sat down with the Lord to count the cost, I realized that although it was a good price, the land purchase and building project would stretch us a bit too much and might put the ministry in jeopardy. The large building that we would build on the land would include enormous maintenance, utility, and staffing requirements. I was willing to go for it if the Lord gave the green light, but after prayer, we decided to take a smaller and wiser step at that time. Whatever you sign for you must care for. Count the cost.

Debt Cancellation

I have seen God perform miracles for people who had huge debt loads. I have seen Him clear many bills, loans, and charges suddenly. One family I know had over $60,000 in credit card bills dissolved within a month period. Another family had all their debt (over $30,000 worth) dissolved overnight. Others have had finances supernaturally given to them for debt payment in meetings we have attended.

Sometimes however, God will hold back on the miracles of debt cancellation, and instead teach wisdom, discipline, and stewardship. I know individuals who have received provisional miracles a number of times and yet have still not learned wisdom and restraint. They continue to go back into debt.

If you are in debt right now, I definitely would pray for a miracle, but I would also begin immediately operating in the wisdom and restraint of the Spirit. Don't say in your heart, "Oh, if God will pay off my bills, I will never get back in debt again," and then go out and charge a meal on a credit card. That is a sure sign that you have no intention of changing. Make a quality decision

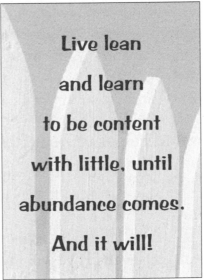

Live lean and learn to be content with little, until abundance comes. And it will!

to change right now. Invite the Lord to show you how you can walk through the situation you are in even if it takes a number of years. Allow the Lord Himself to be your fulfillment – and not your next hamburger or your next new jacket or boots. Live lean and learn to be content with little, until abundance comes. And it will! Paul said that he learned to be content in whatever state he was in – leanness or abundance (see Philippians 4:11).

Do whatever you can to fulfill your commitments, and use discretion to make your life easier for yourself. For example, look for ways you can trim your budget. Remove everything in your life that is not a necessity if you are suffering with a debt load that is heavy to bear. Perhaps look at ways to combine loans and charges into one manageable payment, or consult with a godly financial counselor. You might have to work more than one job and make sacrifices as you move toward your goal. Make it your passion and your focus to dissolve your debt. Do whatever it takes. Humble yourself and diligently apply yourself to get it cleared up. While you are applying diligence, believe God for your miracle and for supernatural intervention as well.

Miracles of Debt Removal and Bill Payment

In Elisha's day, there was a widow who was in big-time debt. She was in so much debt that she said to Elisha, "The creditor has come to take my two children to be his slaves" (2 Kings 4:1). Elisha asked her what she had in the house (remember, the Lord will always use what you have even if it seems like it is nothing.) She replied, "Your maidservant has nothing in the house except a jar of oil."

The prophet started with what she had and instructed her to go borrow some empty vessels from the neighbors. She acquired all she could find, shut the door behind her, and poured oil into all the vessels as she was told (see 2 Kings 4:3-6). After she filled all the vessels and there were no vessels left, the oil stopped. Elisha then said, "Go, sell the oil and pay your debt, and you and your sons can live on the rest" (2 Kings 4:7).

The Lord is the same today as He was then. What do you have to work with right now? Don't focus on what you do not have, but discover what you do have. She was diligent to obtain the vessels, pour the oil, and sell it. This woman didn't wait for a miracle to fall out of heaven. She applied herself. This is a true key. She didn't whine in bitterness over her life and think, "Oh, I am just a single mom and life is so hard. No one supports me and now my children will be taken." No! When she heard the Word of the Lord, she acted on it. She diligently obeyed the Word.

Sometimes bitterness of heart can keep the miracle dimension at bay. Everyone has hard times in life. Life is not usually easy for anyone unless you choose to create ease through the grace of God in the midst of your hard places. When difficulties come, you either allow them to be stumbling blocks for you or you make them stepping stones toward your breakthrough and testimony. It is your choice. There is no room for self-pity if you desire to live in the miracle realm. Bitterness and self-pity

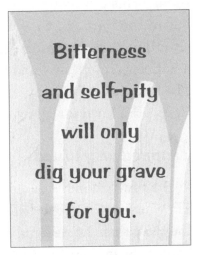

Bitterness and self-pity will only dig your grave for you.

will only dig your grave for you, and you will have no one to hold responsible for your final state except yourself. This widow stepped out of self-pity into her miracle by aligning with the Word and doing something about her situation. Her miracle was just around the corner.

One of our team leaders and itinerant ministers, Melissa Fisher, had suffered in a very difficult marriage prior to coming to Christ. In the marriage there were some unwise financial decisions that brought about some heavy debt. When the marriage terminated, her husband made some choices that left Melissa carrying the debt load. She was upset and hurt about this. After she came to Christ, she forgave her ex-husband but was still stuck with the debt – $32,000. Her heart was heavy, but she went into prayer and cried out to God. She had come to know that God was a miracle worker and she needed a miracle of debt cancellation.

After prayer, she contacted the IRS and they sent her some forms to fill out and return. She did complete the forms, but in the natural, they did not look like they applied to her situation. A month after she returned the forms, she received a notice saying they had chosen to cancel $26,500 of the debt. The IRS canceling any amount of debt is indeed a miracle! Praise the Lord for His goodness!

Trapped or trained

I knew two individuals who got trapped in a Ponzi scheme. They both lost a great deal of money in the investment; in fact, they lost their homes and their life savings, and were left with bank debt in addition to their other losses. It was tragic. One of them forgave the individuals who deceived him, and he and his wife decided to lay their lives on the altar before God once again. They acknowledged their loss and definitely grieved over it, but they decided to move on, living each day in fullness.

They downsized everything and diligently started over. In a few years their heads were above water again and God was helping them rebuild their lives. They did see some small miracles along the way for which they were thankful, but the process was mainly slow and steady. They decided not to look back, choosing instead to find their joy in the midst of it all. They allowed the situation to train them to live as overcomers.

The other couple handled their devastation differently. They could not forgive the friend who had encouraged them to invest, nor could they forgive the company owner who was responsible for the scheme. Their hearts were very bitter and they could not let go of their grief. They borrowed some money to make further investments in a new venture in order to get a quick return on their investment. They actually lost more capital as a result. (Usually opportunities that promise or offer large, quick returns on investments are fairly unstable and unfruitful.) Their marriage relationship became strained and their health was compromised due to the stress. They had already lost their financial security due to the investment that went bad, but because of their reaction to it, they also lost their peace and joy in life.

No matter what loss you have suffered, the Lord has a recovery program for you. He is totally committed to your financial freedom.

Financial Recovery

The following are some helpful principles that can give you a place to start toward your financial recovery.

1. Surrender your situation to God.

Proverbs 3:5-6 says, "Trust in the Lord with all your heart and do not lean on your own understanding. In all your ways acknowledge Him, and He will make your paths straight."

The old saying, "Let go and let God" fits well here. Don't lean on your own understanding. The situation is probably bigger than you can handle anyway, so give it to God. You have a promise that He will watch over whatever you commit to Him.

2. Take inventory.

Take note of how you got into the situation. You do not want to make the same mistakes again. Think it through carefully and invite the Lord to give you counsel and understanding. Ask Holy Spirit to show you the root causes of the failure. You want to ask the Lord to reveal these things to you so you do not repeat the calamity. Be honest with yourself and take personal responsibility for your situation. Repent from your wrong choices and ask the Lord to forgive you.

3. Forgive yourself and others.

Unforgiveness holds you in emotional and mental torment. Forgive everyone that might have been involved in setting you up for loss. Writing down their names and the way they hurt you is sometimes helpful so you can officially forgive each one. Repent from any bitterness or offense you have toward them. Jesus taught us to forgive from the heart (Matthew 18:21-35). When Jesus taught us to pray, He said,

"Forgive us our debts, **as we also have forgiven** our debtors" (Matthew 6:12, emphasis mine). It is important to forgive others in order to have peace within and to have a clear place in the spirit for God to intervene.

Don't beat yourself up for your mistakes and mismanagement. Remember, you are deeply loved by God and He is on your side. He wants to help you and He will help you. Sometimes we need to forgive ourselves more than anyone else. Forgive yourself.

4. Ask the Lord for His recovery counsel.

During the time David was on the run from King Saul, he lived in the land of the Philistines. After one outing, when David returned home to Ziklag he discovered a great, overwhelming loss – not only to himself, but also to all the men who followed him. When David sought the Lord for counsel, He said, "Pursue, for you will surely overtake them, and you will surely rescue all" (1 Samuel 30:8). David knew exactly what to do. He did it, and without fail he recovered all.

Although David was deeply broken over the tragedy, he did not respond out of his remorse and anguish. He responded out of obedience to the counsel of the Lord. The Lord will grant you wisdom and counsel, but you must wait on Him for it. When you surrender completely to Him, it is easier to hear from Him. Wait in peace, knowing He will give you His plan. His Word might not come to you right away, so wait for it. Read your Bible every day and ask God to speak His counsel and wisdom to you through His Word.

5. Practical diligence.

Do what you can to be diligent and faithful in the little. It is usually much easier to get into debt than it is to get out of it. Diligence, patience, and good wise stewardship will help you finish strong. You might need to get extra employment for a season, or downsize for a few years, in order to get yourself on a strong foundation again. But you can do it! Look for creative ways to pay your debt or make bill payments. Don't be in a hurry, for haste can bring more disaster to you. Walk patiently and diligently before God.

6. Believe for your miracle.

Remember, while you are being faithful and diligent, your complete breakthrough is only one miracle away. Call your bills, "Paid!" When Ron and I were in our "lean years," I remember piling the bills on the table one day and calling them "paid" in Jesus' name. By faith I would write the checks and then wait with expectation for the money to come in to cover them. Then I would mail them off (do not send checks out until you have the money to cover the expense). I was amazed at how quickly those bills were paid. I called them *paid* every day until they were completely paid in the natural.

Peter put Jesus in an awkward position concerning the payment of taxes. In order to avoid offending the people, Jesus told Peter to go catch a fish and find a coin in the mouth of the fish he caught – enough for payment for both of them (see Matthew 17:24-27). That is a fun miracle! God can do this for you, too. Believe for your miracle! Expect a miracle! You never know where you will find the finances you need.

7. *Praise and be thankful.*

One thing I have learned is that murmuring and complaining will always block the miracle provision of God. But praise and thanksgiving opens the way for supernatural provision.

Years ago on the mission field I was in charge of the kitchen. I prepared three meals every day for about fifty people. When I was given the position, the leadership informed me that I had a "faith budget." In other words, there was nothing much in the natural – I had to *believe* for food to cook. They gave me a little money to cover a few essentials, but it was slim pickings for sure.

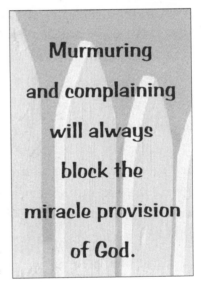

Murmuring and complaining will always block the miracle provision of God.

I tried my best and attempted to be as creative as possible, but oh my! I seemed to be in trouble all the time. We had a high carbohydrate and low protein diet, as those types of foods were available at lower cost. The problem was that the women got fat on the carbs and the guys got skinny due to the low protein. There were complaints on a regular basis about the food, and I felt terrible. The more I prayed and tried to cook nice meals, the more everyone complained and the tighter the provision was.

One day I was making bread and crying out to God. "Why am I not getting breakthrough in provision?" He answered,

"It is because of the murmuring and complaining." He assured me that He had more than enough provision, but the negativity was hindering Him from releasing it. We had actually brassed over the heavens with our complaints.

I quickly shared with the others what the Lord revealed, and there was a time of repentance. The whole camp was now praising and thanking God for every mouthful of food rather than grumbling. Within twenty-four hours the miracles began! That is when Bessy, the cow, showed up – a gift from a local farmer. We had to learn to milk her, but from that day on we had loads of fresh milk, cream, and butter. It was wonderful.

The very next day, a local butcher began to give us 15 kilos (over 30 pounds) of hamburger per week. This was a major blessing for all, since we did not have much meat in our diet – except for a special chicken dinner once a month and an iguana that I pressure-cooked whenever "Jungle Joe" (a young man in our school) shot one for us. Our team, however, was not at all fond of the lizard meat, so everyone was elated with the generous, weekly portion of hamburger meat!

Food was coming in from every direction once we praised and thanked the Lord for all things. What a difference it made. Our breakthrough literally came overnight. So can yours!

8. Give your way out of debt.

I will cover the subject of *sowing* in detail later, but you can sow your way out of debt if you intentionally give towards your debt cancellation or bill payment. Ron and I have paid off homes this way. We have intentionally given financial gifts for the Lord's buildings and reaped for our own.

One time we had a car repair bill of close to $500. That might not seem much to you, but at the time it could just as well have been five million, since we did not have any extra funds at all. One night we were giving into an offering and had only five dollars to our name. We intentionally gave the five dollars in faith and believed for the $500 repair bill to be paid. Within two days, the money came in and we paid the bill off.

9. Create a plan.

If you live within your means, you will not get in over your head again. The next time you feel a temptation to go on a spending spree that is outside of your budget, remember the mess you lived in as a result of that pattern in the past. The pleasure of the spree is short-lived. Make some long-term as well as short-term financial goals and work toward achieving them.

In your plan, work out your budget for your current needs and also have a savings plan where you put money away to fulfill a longer-term goal. It is helpful to create a separate account for that. You will be surprised how the savings account can grow simply by putting a little money into it each month. You also might want to have a container to put all your change in at the end of the day, and once a month deposit it into your savings account. This can really add up when God puts His blessing on it.

Dream about what it will be like to be debt free. Dream of a plan to get out of debt and keep that dream before you. Live the dream.

10. Get ready for breakthrough!

I have absolute faith for your debt and bill cancellation and am praying for you. May you expect and experience the miracle intervention of God. Get excited! Stir up expectation within you. God is about ready to do something great for YOU. He wants to establish you in His wisdom and His breakthrough for the rest of your life ... and He will! Instead of being the borrower, you will be the lender. Breakthrough! Breakthrough! Breakthrough! It is on its way!

Chapter 4

MESSENGERS OF

PROVISION

Chapter 4

MESSENGERS OF PROVISION

You don't have to feel alone when believing for your financial breakthrough. God will work with you to establish you in truth and wisdom. But it is important to know that He also has some amazing help for you! Holy Spirit is always at your side and is truly your Helper in all things. He will work with you to secure provision. He will teach you the ways of truth concerning Kingdom prosperity. He also has other helpers available to serve you.

Angels of Provision

In Hebrews 1:14, you are taught that God has assigned angels to serve you. They can help you in matters of provision. A number of years ago, our ministry had been given an assignment by God to fulfill. It required what seemed like a large amount of finance at that time. We were in prayer one morning, as we had a deadline to meet that week and there was no provision in sight. While engaged in prayer, the Lord spoke distinctly to my heart, "I am dispatching angels from the provision department in heaven to your ministry. Call them in from the north, the south, the east, and the west."

We were so excited! We responded to the word by calling forth the angels in Jesus' name and dispatching them to fetch the provision that was needed. Our need was met almost immediately. Within a couple of days every dollar we required for the fulfillment of that assignment, and more, was in hand.

A prophet that I trust told me once that when the Lord assigns angels to you, they are assigned for life. I liked that but asked him, "Where is that in the Word?" He responded, "For the gifts and the calling of God are irrevocable" (Romans 11:29). I decided to agree with the Word on that one! Those angels are still working with us today, bringing in provision to fulfill the work we are called to in Christ.

Elijah had angels provide food for him just after his victory over the prophets of Baal at Mount Carmel. After the Lord sent fire from heaven to prove that He was God, Elijah had the 450 prophets of Baal executed. To escape Jezebel's death threat, Elijah ran into the wilderness. He prayed that he might die and said, "It is enough; now, O Lord, take my life" (1 Kings 19:4). As he slept, an angel came to Elijah and provided a cake baked on coals to eat and a jar of water for drink. The angel returned a second time and told him to eat and drink again. The Bible says, "So he arose and ate and drank, and went in the strength of that food forty days and forty nights to Horeb, the mountain of God" (verse 8). There he met with God and received important instructions. The angel of provision played a critical role at the start of the next phase of Elijah's ministry.

How to Dispatch Angels

Psalm 103:20 gives us the key to dispatching angels:

Bless the Lord, you His angels, mighty in strength, who perform His word, obeying the voice of His word!

Angels are not required to obey man. They obey the Lord and carry out the Lord's Word. You give voice to the Word of God and angels then carry it out. When the Lord quickens His Word to you and you respond by decreeing that Word, angels are dispatched to fulfill it.

Lost Articles

We have seen God miraculously restore lost articles many times. When my oldest son was seven years old, we were in Mexico on an outreach and he found an emerald on the beach. It meant a lot to him and we were convinced that God gave it as a special confirmation of His love. It was beautiful and we all rejoiced over his find. He put it in his pocket during the day and placed it on the counter in our van at night. He loved it. The third day of our trip he lost the emerald. This was disturbing to all of us, as we knew how much it meant to him. We searched everywhere for it and prayed, but could not find it. After we returned to Canada, I was saying prayers with him one night, and there was the emerald right on his bedside table. We had no idea where it came from, but were convinced the Lord sent an angel to deliver it to him. There was no other explanation.

God's Unusual Messengers of Provision

Never underestimate what God can do, or try to predict how He will do it. He can use unusual messengers to provide for you.

In 1 Kings 17:2-8, God sent the ravens to bring Elijah bread and meat in the morning and evening while he was at the brook Cherith. Elijah had no food available to him at the brook other than what the Lord sent through the ravens. Perhaps God will choose vessels that might seem a little strange to you.

God Uses People as His Messengers

Even though the Lord is able to meet our needs miraculously, He often likes to use people to meet the needs of others. He loves our partnership with Him and will often nudge us to help others meet their needs. I love being used by Him like this!

During the season that Ron and I were struggling financially, I had need of some winter clothes. We had come back from YWAM in Hawaii in the spring, so I didn't need winter clothes until winter arrived. It was getting cold and I prayed for some warm clothes. One day I opened my door and there was a box of clothes, including a new warm winter coat. Everything fit perfectly. Now, perhaps an angel dropped that box of clothes off, or maybe it was an "angel" with skin.

Milk

On another occasion in the same season, I went to the fridge to get my children some milk, and there was not a drop of it to be found. Momentarily, I complained within, as I was discouraged. However, the Spirit of God rose up within me and said, "Do not murmur or complain. Praise Me!" I began to praise the Lord immediately. I turned on the water tap and thanked Him for the water we had available to us. I filled two glasses with water, one for each son, and prayed, "Lord, You turned water into wine, so You can certainly turn water into milk."

I set the water before the boys and believed that it would turn to milk as they drank it. I gave thanks to God for everything I saw in our cupboards – every plate, cup, utensil, and can of food. After about twenty minutes of praising Him, the doorbell rang. It was a woman I had met only casually previously, and she was standing there with a gallon jar full of fresh farm milk.

She said, "I feel rather awkward about this, but I was up at the farm getting my milk and felt the Lord wanted me to get you a gallon. Can you use it?"

Oh my! My praise had worked a release of provision. God chose this wonderful, obedient woman to meet the need. Not only did we get the milk we needed, it was the best – fresh from the cow!

Stranded on I-5

I was on my way to Tijuana, Mexico, with a team of youth when our vehicle broke down on the highway. A tire had blown and my husband was not with us. None of the young people knew what to do, nor did I. I pulled off to the side of the highway and began to pray, "Lord, send help ... PLEASE!!" I hate to admit this, but I did not even know where the spare was. We had been stopped just a few minutes when a pickup truck pulled over. A man came out of the vehicle and said in a southern accent, "Looks like you need your tire changed!" Without giving me time to respond, he went to the back of his truck and took out his tools —PLUS a brand new tire – the exact size we needed. In moments he had changed the tire.

He was putting his tools away while I was checking to see how the young people were doing. I was elated. When I turned to thank him and ask what I could give him in payment for the tire, he had disappeared. He was long gone. Perhaps he was an angel, or maybe a hand-chosen vessel that God desired to use.

On our trips to Tijuana we had many breakdowns and witnessed God's goodness every time. He is faithful!

Messengers of Provision Via the Mailbox

My husband and I have often been pleasantly surprised when we pick up the mail and find special messages of encouragement, and sometimes breakthrough provision, awaiting us. So often the provision will be the exact amount to the penny that we need at a given time. We know it is more than coincidence. Often the provision has come from people we have never met. One time when we tried to follow up, our letter of thanks was returned to sender as "undeliverable." Perhaps the provision came from an angel or ... a messenger with skin on who moves a lot.

To finish this chapter, I'm going to include a story by our good friend and ministry companion, Steve Shultz, founder of the Elijah List (a significant global prophetic portal in our day). He experienced a surprise encounter of provision when he went to his mailbox one day. As you read, remember that God has these "messengers of provision" for you, too!

Here is his story:

My wife and I were hurting badly financially as the Elijah List was getting going. Initially, I had never expected it to ever be an official ministry, as it was simply a hobby for me. My previous business had totally failed and I was discouraged, feeling like a loser at every level!

But if there were any area where I felt the least successful, it would have been in the area of finances. My dad always was bad at finances so he never taught me a thing about it. Although I saw his mistakes, I didn't seem to learn from them. God was about to give me a "school'n" such as I had never seen.

During that difficult time, around the time of my birthday that August, God told me to ask Him for whatever I wanted for my birthday. I asked for breakthrough in finances. Well, August came and went. Nothing. By

October, I anxiously explained to my wife Derene, "If we don't get $5,000 today, we'll lose our car, our house, and everything!" Our only option was to move back into my in-law's house. How humiliating that would be! We knew they loved us and would help us in crisis, but we were very embarrassed to be in that situation.

Soon after, I woke up one morning with the "Happy Birthday" song on my mind. At that time, our ministry had only hundreds of readers, not the 400,000+ (email and Web) we have today.

As I drove my car later that day, the radio announcer shared some trivia regarding the day in history that the "Happy Birthday" song was copyrighted. My jaw dropped.

Soon after, I drove to the post office to get the mail. Only one envelope was in our mailbox that day and it was a check. We had done no fundraising. This check was from someone I had never heard of. It was EXACTLY $5,000 to the penny. This gift is what launched the Elijah List's expansion from a hobby into a viable ministry. A messenger of provision was chosen by God to help us at this critical point.

The breakthrough came in the spirit when I asked Him in August and manifested in the natural around two months later. Clearly God gets to pick our birthdays as well as our moment of breakthrough. The rest is history.

STEVE SHULTZ
The Elijah List

Chapter 5

FINANCIAL GROWTH
– GOD'S WAY

Chapter 5

FINANCIAL GROWTH – GOD'S WAY

The Bible gives very clear instruction on how to prosper. It is easy if you carefully and joyfully follow God's handbook for success. In this chapter, I will share with you some principles that I have followed ever since I became a Christian. When we obey the Word of God, we prosper. When we disobey, we suffer consequences. Choosing God's ways is wise, as His supreme laws govern success no matter what is occurring in worldly economy. These glorious principles work!

The First and the Best Go to God!

The Scriptures clearly teach us that the first and the best of all, given with a sincere heart of love and faith, go to God. When we honor Him with the first and the best, then heaven opens over us, and benefits bless our life. The tithe, which means 10 percent, belongs to the Lord. Genesis 14:18-20 records when the tithe was first offered by Abraham to Melchizedek, king of Salem and "priest of God Most High" (perhaps he was the pre-incarnate Christ, eternal high priest). God was delighted in this act and blessed Abraham as a result. Later, this act was made law so that all of Israel would live in the same blessing as Abraham.

In the New Testament we are not under a law to give 10 percent, but we offer the tithe through the Kingdom love law and offer it from the heart. The blessings of the tithe then come upon us. Malachi 3:10-12 says:

> "Bring the whole tithe into the storehouse, so that there may be food in My house, and test Me now in this," says the Lord of hosts, "if I will not open for you the windows of heaven and pour out for you a blessing until it overflows. Then I will rebuke the devourer for you, so that it will not destroy the fruits of the ground; nor will your vine in the field cast its grapes," says the Lord of hosts. "All the nations will call you blessed, for you shall be a delightful land," says the Lord of hosts.

Look at the blessings that are promised you as a result of tithing:

1. He will open the heavens over your life.

2. He'll pour out a blessing you won't have room to contain.

3. He will rebuke the devourer on your behalf.

4. Your fruitfulness will not be lost.

5. The nations will call you blessed.

6. You will be a delightful land.

From the time I was saved, I tithed. Immediately after receiving Christ I had the desire to give Him my all. For over 35 years I have never missed giving my tithe. This is because I know the value of it. When you tithe you are saying, "God, You are more important to me than anything in life!" In Malachi, we are taught that the tithe belongs to the Lord and He actually rebuked Israel when they withheld it from Him. He said that they were robbing Him by neglecting tithes and offerings (Malachi 3:8-9).

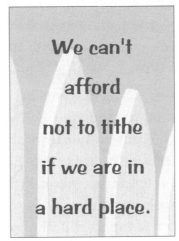

We can't afford not to tithe if we are in a hard place.

Can I Afford It?

I have heard many say that they cannot afford to tithe when they are tight for finances. I personally do not believe this. In fact, we can't afford not to tithe if we are in a hard place. I would rather give the Lord what belongs to Him and do without myself. Where your treasure is, that is where your heart is also. Even in the most difficult times, we continued to give God the first and best. It belongs to Him.

Here is a scenario. An investor came into partnership with a bankrupt individual who had no money to invest and no assets. He said, "I will give all that I have into this investment and all I want is the first 10 percent return on the gross. You can have the remaining 90 percent and you can manage the account." What a glorious partnership for the bankrupt individual. He was obviously happy about that exchange, as anyone would be. He made no investment, had a promise of success, and received 90 percent of the gross profit. The investor gave everything into the investment.

When it was time for the individual to give the investor his 10 percent, he decided that he couldn't fulfill it that month. He had used his 90 percent to repair his vehicle, pay the rent and utilities, buy some new clothes, buy some items on the Internet, and pay off some bills. After that, although he found he was a little short for the rest of the month, he took his family out for a movie and some pizza, and he bought an advanced satellite package for his television. After all, he deserved to have a bit of pleasure – he worked hard and had done without in the past! He thought he would wait until the next month and catch up then, but a similar scenario happened the next month and the next month. He got used to spending the investor's money each month.

After a year, the investor came for his 10 percent. The individual explained that he was sorry but he could not afford to pay him the 10 percent. Now, let me ask you, "What would you do if you were the investor?" Not only is withholding the 10 percent illegal embezzlement, but it is completely selfish and foolish. He had the perfect business partner, a dream-come-true, and he blew it!

Jesus is like the investor. He gave His entire life – all He was and all He had. We are like the bankrupt individual – dead in our trespasses and sin.

I have heard people say, "Yes, but it is my money. I worked for it." If that is your take on it, then you have not truly given your life to Jesus. When we come to Christ, there is an exchange. He gives you His life and you give Him yours. All that He is and has is yours, and all that you are and have becomes His.

My life is no longer my own. It belongs to Him. When I tithe I establish that truth, because I realize that my life fully belongs to Him. What an awesome blessing that He only asks for 10 percent. Investors in the world would never offer that kind of deal. They would never give you something for nothing, let alone offer you 90 percent of the income.

Most governments ask for much more than 10 percent and do not give anywhere near as much in return. Yet the King of all kings only asks for 10 percent. The reason the Lord calls the first 10 percent His is so you will then engage in the fullness of His blessings. He definitely does not need the money that you give Him, but you need His partnership so all that is left in your hand comes under His blessing and multiplication.

During our personal financial testing season, we never withheld the tithe. I remember saying to God one day that

I would rather do without everything than withhold what was due Him. It was truly a difficult season for a while, even though we were faithful in our tithes. But then after a few years, the blessings came in on every wave and still do.

Through the test we saw what was in our heart. We discovered through the trials that our love for God was stronger than anything that money could possibly buy. I believe that the prosperity we enjoy today is based on our faithfulness in tithing. Tithing in some ways is one of the most powerful expressions of worship. Over the years we have put our faith out to tithe more and more. We went from one tithe to two tithes, then three, and continued to increase. I love tithing and I love the benefits!

Sowing

If you want abundance, then Kingdom economy requires that you sow what you desire to reap. It is a very easy principle and the Bible is full of confirmation. I have seen it work for many years in every area of my life. God made a perpetual promise in Genesis 8:22, "While the earth remains, seedtime and harvest ... shall not cease." The earth still remains, so the promise is still good. If you sow a seed there will be a corresponding harvest.

The principle of sowing and reaping is very easy to grasp. If I plant bean seeds in a natural garden, I will grow beans (not corn). If I plant many bean seeds, I will reap more beans than if I just planted a few. If I sow my seeds into good, rich soil, I will reap bountifully. When I plant my seed and it grows to a full plant, it has more seed inside the fruit.

The soil that you sow into is important. I always look for soil that is conducive to Kingdom advancement. If you sow finances into good soil, you will receive an abundant harvest of finances. I look for ministries to sow into that are rich in faith, love and character. When I sow into anointed ministries, I am assured that the seed will be used for Kingdom advancement. I have always increased in finance as a result of sowing financial seed, but I have also increased in the anointing of the ministry that I sow into.

> You need His partnership so all that is left in your hand comes under His blessing and multiplication.

You can sow your way into prosperity and abundance. You can sow your way out of debt. I know because I have lived by this Kingdom principle for over 35 years in my personal life, our businesses, and our ministries!

Our ministry needed to build a new studio. It was approximately a one million dollar project. We were about to move forward with fundraising when a burden to build a home for abused children in Asia came to our attention. We were so touched by the need, and felt to sow into the home rather than start the fundraising for our own building. I told the missionary that we would build the home for him. We needed $100,000 to cover the building cost and the care of the children for the first year. God blessed us as we raised the money, and we were able to disburse the entire amount for the building. As a result, we now have over 30 children rescued from being child soldiers in Asia. They are safe in the arms of Jesus.

We then wanted to proceed with our own project, but another need came up. This time a friend of ours was trying to purchase a building in Cambodia that could house girls coming out of the sex trade, so we raised another $100,000 for that need. Then, a family on our team felt led to move to Africa to help orphans. They needed to raise $60,000 to cover their move, so we committed to sowing into them and covering that need.

Every time we desired to move forward to raise funds for our building, needs for the poor came to our attention. Our team in Thailand felt an urgent need to build a shelter for children coming out of the sex trade, so we committed to that need and met it. At the same time, many of our ministry friends were engaged in building projects so we sowed something into everyone who asked.

Finally, the Lord gave us the go-ahead to raise finances for the new studio that would create Christian media to be broadcast all over the world. We had nothing to start with, as we had sown and sown and sown our precious seed into good soil. When you add it all up and multiply it by a hundredfold, that is a great deal of finance – more than what we needed. We had absolute confidence in moving forward with our building. We stood in faith and called forth the return on the seed we had sown into all those building projects. This is how dreams become realities. Sow with purpose and intention to receive your return.

Seed to Sow

In order to obtain a harvest, you need seed to sow. The Scripture teaches us that God furnishes seed to the sower and will even multiply the seed (2 Corinthians 9:10). If you truly want to sow but you don't have seed, then simply ask the Lord for seed to sow. He will give it to you. Sometimes I hear people say, "Oh, if only I had some money, I would care for the poor." Well, ask for the seed to sow. If you really want to, God will give it to you. He has never failed me yet when I have asked Him for seed. Just remember not to eat your seed. If you eat your seed, there is none left to grow a harvest for you. If you ask for seed and it comes into your hand, then sow it – do not spend it. When you sow your seed, it will produce bread for you to eat and it will provide more seed for you.

One of the ways I have helped people out of poverty is to give them a seed to sow when they tell me they have nothing. I always emphasize: DO NOT SPEND THIS SEED. SOW IT. This is because I know that if they sow in faith according to the Word of God they will increase. If they give from their increase, then they will reap even more.

Reaping

Many have grasped the principle of sowing and they are faithful sowers. Intentional reaping, however, is also extremely vital in order to be blessed with abundance. What would you think of a farmer who loved to sow but was shy about reaping, or perhaps even resistant to it? He joyfully and abundantly throws his seed out into a field and says, "Yippy,

I LOVE sowing!!! I don't care about the reaping. I just love to sow! Yippy!" If you were an onlooker, you would think he was an absolute lunatic.

Here is another scenario: A farmer faithfully sows seed into his field. It is good ground and the seed grows him an abundant harvest. But harvest time comes and goes. You drive by weekly and watch the neglected harvest rot and die. One day you meet the farmer while shopping in town and ask him why he didn't reap the field. "Oh," he says, "If God wants me to have a harvest, He will give me one. I am just going to be a faithful sower."

What?!? That makes no sense. God did give him the harvest. It was right in front of his eyes every day, but he failed to put the sickle in the ground and reap.

In a spiritual sense it is the same. You sow by faith *and* you must also intentionally reap by faith. Many Christians are faithful in sowing but are not aware of reaping. Some are actually resistant to reaping, as they feel it might be ungodly to actually desire a harvest. I have heard a few actually make comments like the farmers in the stories above. They will say things like, "If God wants me to have a return on my sowing, He will give it," or, "I love sowing and sacrificing, but I don't care if I get any return." These responses make no sense whatsoever and are definitely not going to bring forth the fruit of abundance. A farmer sows with the intention to reap, and so should you. When you sow faithfully into good ground, a harvest awaits you. Believe for it.

Reap in the time of harvest

Some people get discouraged when they sow one day and don't reap the next. There is a time for sowing and a time for reaping. Let your seed grow. I have found that some of the seeds I sowed almost twenty years ago are still bearing fruit today. They are perennials! Some seeds produce a harvest very quickly while others take time. It is like that in the natural, too. Some vegetables, like Swiss chard, produce a quick harvest in a number of weeks, but an apple tree will take a few years.

Be patient and wait for your harvest. Don't dig up your seed every day to see if it is producing. It will! Second Corinthians 9:6-11 declares:

> Now this I say, he who sows sparingly will also reap sparingly, and he who sows bountifully will also reap bountifully. Each one must do just as he has purposed in his heart, not grudgingly or under compulsion, for God loves a cheerful giver. And God is able to make all grace abound to you, so that always having all sufficiency in everything, you may have an abundance for every good deed; as it is written, "HE SCATTERED ABROAD, HE GAVE TO THE POOR, HIS RIGHTEOUSNESS ENDURES FOREVER." Now He who supplies seed to the sower and bread for food will supply and multiply your seed for sowing and increase the harvest of your righteousness; you will be enriched in everything for all liberality, which through us is producing thanksgiving to God.

Birthing Your Return

There are a number of breakthrough principles we can learn from the story of when Elijah confronted the prophets of Baal on Mount Carmel (1 Kings 18:19-40).

1. **Restore your devotion to God.** When it was Elijah's turn to call on the name of his God, he first restored the broken altar. This speaks of restoring devotion to Christ. In Elijah's day, the people of God had backslidden from their devotion. This was a prophetic act to call the nation back into pure worship and service. If you desire sustained breakthrough in finances, then make sure you have sustained, unwavering devotion to God.

2. **Sow extravagantly.** He then sowed a very extravagant offering according to what he was believing for. The land had been in a severe drought and famine for years. The nation needed water, but the people also needed to be restored to God. Elijah placed an offering of an ox on the altar and called for an offering of water. What? Water? Yes! He was believing for water (rain), so he sowed water. He drenched the sacrifice and filled the trenches with 12 measures of water. Everything was saturated with water. This was a huge offering. Why did he sow it? Because, he was believing for a massive return.

After the water filled the trenches, Elijah called on God. God answered and received the offering with fire. He licked it all up. He took it all. Have you ever said to the Lord something like, "Oh Lord, I give you all that I am and all that I have," and He took it? Well, that is what happened

108

here. God answered by fire and received the offering – all of it. Sometimes we do not see the sign of the return on our offering right away and we wonder if the principles of God work. Oh, yes, they do! They surely do!

3. **Posture yourself to birth the fulfillment through prayer.** After the offering was consumed, Elijah heard the sound of a heavy rain (1 Kings 18:41). There was not a drop of water in sight, but he knew the sound in his spirit of what was promised. He went up to the top of Mount Carmel "and he crouched down on the earth and put his face between his knees" (verse 42). This was a birthing position. He had given the offering, he heard the sound of the promised return within his spirit, and then he postured himself to birth the fulfillment of the return through prayer. This is a biblical pattern. God gives the promise to our heart and then we birth it into the earth through faith and prayer until it manifests.

We find an example of this in the New Testament where Anna the prophetess prayed day and night in the temple for over 60 years. The promise of the Messiah had been given in the Old Testament, but it needed to be birthed into the realm of time through prayer. She (along with others in that day) knew the prophetic promise and gave release to it through their focused fasting and prayer (see Luke 2:36-38).

Elijah remained in prayer while he sent his servant to look for the cloud that carried the rain. His servant returned, declaring that there was not a cloud to be found.

Elijah was sure of the promise of God and would not give up. He had given the offering and he knew with confidence there would be a return. He had the Word from God and he stood on it with unwavering faith. Seven times Elijah told his servant to go back (1 Kings 18:43) as he was fully committed to ONLY believe the promise of God. He had no room for doubt.

Sometimes we waver in our faith. But we must stand and not be moved by outward circumstances, as God is faithful. Finally on the seventh time, his servant returned with a good report. He said, "There is a small cloud about the size of a man's hand coming up from the sea." Elijah knew that was his breakthrough, even though it was very small at first. Sometimes your breakthrough does seem small and insignificant in the beginning, but that is your sign that more is coming. Elijah prepared for the great outpouring and it surely came. So will yours!

Sowing in Difficult Times

Sowing financial seed into the Kingdom of God can actually give you breakthrough in difficult times. Even as Elijah sowed water in a time when he most needed water, so also did Isaac sow a sacrificial offering in a time of need. In Genesis 26:1-2 we find that there was a famine in the land. When times are difficult, many tighten their purse strings. Isaac however, sowed in this time of famine. Why? Because he believed that his God was a covenant-keeping God and would continue to be faithful in good times and in bad. When you are in covenant with God, you are blessed all the time because He is so good! Because Isaac believed in the goodness of God, he did not go down to Egypt, but he sowed in the time of famine and God blessed his offering. In that year he reaped a hundredfold return (verse 12).

Sow your way into freedom. Take the little seed that you have and sow it in faith for a harvest. Remember, if you do not have enough to meet your need, then it is seed.

Goals for your Financial Future

Do you have goals for your financial future? Without a clear vision, your money will not work for you. Money is not an end in itself, but is a means to an end. Take time to dream a little. What would you like your life to look like five years from now? Make a list of your dreams. Look over the list and allow the Holy Spirit to give you what I call the "green light of grace." This is an inner witness from God. This witness of the Holy Spirit comes from inside your heart. It feels like clearance and usually stirs within you faith to move ahead. It is a sign that God is with you.

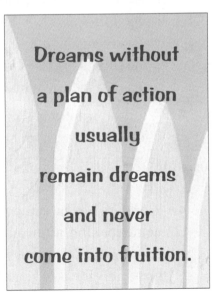

Dreams without a plan of action usually remain dreams and never come into fruition.

Take those dreams that have God's blessing on them and meditate on them further. Ask yourself which one is the most important to you. Take that particular dream and ask

God for a plan of action to fulfill it. Dreams without a plan of action usually remain dreams and never come into fruition. But you can do all things through Christ who strengthens you.

My husband and I desired to go on a missions outreach. We calculated the expenses and it was going to cost us approximately $2,500. That was a lot of money for us during that season in our life. We prayed into the dream and felt God's pleasure on it, so we asked God to help us create a plan of action. Many ideas came to us. It was exciting. We had only three months to raise the $2,500, so here was our plan of action:

1. Fast and pray two days a week and save the grocery money for those two days. Over three months that would give us a savings of around $250. It would give us some extra prayer power, too!

2. Host a garage sale. Not only did this help us raise the needed funds, but it helped us clean our home of things we were not using. People in our church also gave us some things to sell when they discovered it was for a missions outreach. We made over $500 at the garage sale.

3. Window washing. We went from door to door with a bucket and cleaners and asked people if we could wash their windows for a donation. Over the three months, this provided another $500.

4. Work an extra temporary job. At the time, I was at home looking after our young children. I asked a local restaurant if they needed some additional help and they hired me for occasional shifts on a temporary basis. I

usually worked four- or five-hour shifts, and only when my husband was home with the children. With my wage plus tips, I usually made around $100 per shift. In the two months I was on call, I made over $1,000.

5. Collection of soft drink bottles and cans. At that time, we could receive between $.02 and $.07 per bottle for recycling. When we were on our way for groceries or at the park with the kids, we would look for recyclables. We made $200 in three months.

6. Car Wash. My husband and I sponsored a car wash for donations and made another $200 in half a day.

7. Odd jobs. My husband made up a little advertisement and went door to door letting people know that he could help them with odd jobs (i.e., mowing lawns, sweeping driveways, light mechanical work, home maintenance, etc.). He did get a couple of jobs and made around $150.

Every time we collected money, we put it into the savings jar for our trip. You might think, "Well, what is $150 or $200?" By itself, it was not enough to meet the need. But because we had a clear goal and plan of action, it all worked to the fulfillment of our dream. We went on the outreach with more than what we needed.

If you don't have a clear dream and a plan of action to fulfill it, then you have nothing to work toward. You will therefore lack motivation and fall short in the stewardship of your finances.

Serving God on that outreach is now part of our history in Him because we had a clear goal. I knew of others who wanted to go on that missions trip but were waiting for the money to come to them, and it didn't. They wrote some support letters, but very few responded. We did not ask anyone for support money, and yet before we left many had given us some. They had seen our diligence and responded. God rewarded our focus and passion.

Goal setting and creating a clear plan of action is how we run successful businesses and ministries as well.

Faithful Financial Stewardship

The book of Proverbs teaches that wisdom enables and empowers us to prosper in many ways. If we love wisdom, we will be blessed. Financial stewardship is very important and I can't stress enough the importance of living within your means while trusting the Lord for increase. He will bless you.

I counsel many young people when they get married to live lean in the beginning of the marriage and save for the things they desire, rather than going into debt. You can have very little and yet be rich.

For example, let's say that you only make $1,500 income per month. You might think, "This is impossible! How can I live on that?" Let me show you. Your tithe is $150. You choose to rent a small basement suite within walking distance of work for $700 per month (including utilities) rather than renting more extravagant living quarters. You choose not to own a car in this season of your life, but you purchase a secondhand bicycle for $50. You cook your own nutritious meals and are wise in your grocery shopping in order to stay within your $200 per month grocery allowance.

You are creative with your social and recreational life by inviting friends over for board games and fellowship rather than going out to movies or other forms of entertainment. You have a cell phone on a basic plan that costs you under $50 per month. You trim down your budget as much as you possibly can and find that you can meet your needs and still have $50 left over each month if you are careful. You put the extra $50 into a savings account.

You pray for God's intervention each day and have an expectation for blessings. God brings all kinds of surprises your way. It might not seem like you are living in prosperity, but you actually are. You are living within your means and you have a bit left over. Biblical prosperity is best defined as having enough to honor God with your tithes and offerings, enough to meet your own needs, and some left over to help meet the needs of others. Once you establish living within your means as a lifestyle, you will always be free from the oppression of poverty, even in seasons when you have very little. This is how you carve out a realm of prosperity to stand in. You are faithfully stewarding what you have, but are setting clear goals for increase and believing God to open doors for promotion and success.

Over time, you will continually increase. Through your diligence and faithfulness, you are carving out a place in the spirit where you are the head and not the tail. You do not live on credit or borrow money thinking you will pay it back later. When a need comes up or a surprise attack, you go to God in prayer and discover the keys to breakthrough in that particular situation. You learn to live in the realm of supernatural provision and you are rewarded for your faithfulness. If you are faithful in the little, you will be given much (Luke 19:17).

I want to emphasize this again: once you carve out a realm of prosperity for your life, it will follow you all your days as you watch over it. It becomes your sphere of authority. That is why millionaires who become established due to their diligence and stewardship quickly recover if they lose everything. Within a short time they usually become millionaires again. This is because they established that realm in their life. Establish your realm of prosperity as early in life as possible. Prosperity is not based on how much money you possess; prosperity is established in the spirit by faithfully and diligently living within your means while believing for increase.

On the other hand...

On the other hand, you can potentially carve out a realm of financial lack and poverty if you get into unnecessary debt and spend beyond your means. Most often, individuals go deeper into debt over the years once they choose the route of living beyond their means. They sometimes think, "I will just overspend this month but will catch up next month." You must break the cycle of overspending or you will always be under the weight of debt and the oppression of lack and poverty.

I know of many who have had their debts completely cleared through an act of grace, and within a short time they are back in the same pit. Some think, "Well, I no longer have other current bills, so I will buy what I want – right now – even though I can't really afford it. It will be easy to pay it off later." That is a trap for sure. They once again carved out a realm of poverty and lack in the spirit due to their choices to live beyond their means.

Start now

If you find yourself in this situation, be encouraged. This cycle can be broken through faithful stewardship of your finances. It takes great discipline and faith, but you can carve out a brand new place of abundance to live in for the rest of your life if you start now. Make the right financial choices today and reap a glorious future tomorrow.

Ask God for wisdom in spending and be faithful in your financial obligations. It is ungodly to fail in fulfilling financial commitments. Keep your commitments. Pay them on time. I have heard people say, "Well, I cannot pay the rent this month as I do not have the money," but they go and buy a new pair of jeans or some hair dye. If you have unpaid rent, then you need to get out and do what it takes to obtain the finance to pay it – even if that means hosting a car wash or cutting your neighbor's grass. Pay your bills and pay them on time.

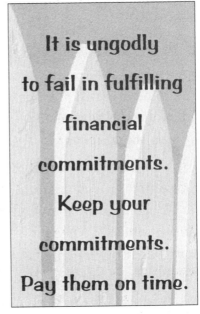

It is ungodly to fail in fulfilling financial commitments. Keep your commitments. Pay them on time.

Faithful stewardship also involves looking after what you have. For example, if you are blessed with some furniture, then look after it. God rewards the faithful. Even if what you have does not look like much, care for it well and steward it with a faithful heart. The Lord will reward you with more.

Ask an Important Question

One important key to help you come into mature financial stewardship is to ask yourself a vital question before you spend money. Here it is: *"Do I really need this?"* You will be surprised how much finance is wasted on "insignificant nothings." Start making a list of all of your spending each day. Every time you spend money, write down the amount and what it is for.

Ideally, it is best to ask the key question before you spend, but even afterwards it helps to go through your list and ask yourself if the money spent was actually worth the pleasure of the moment. If you spend your money for what is meaningful to the fulfillment of your goals, your money will work for you in amazing ways.

I worked with a friend on this principle. She discovered through financial tracking that she was "throwing away" over $350 per month on meaningless things that she could easily do without. $350 per month is $4,200 per year. That could pay for a vacation or some new furniture. It could pay off a vehicle or provide closing costs on a home purchase.

Coffee and lunches

It is amazing how the daily latte at the coffee shop or a quick meal at a local fast-food restaurant can add up. It is probably more advantageous to your budget to make your coffee and lunches at home, and they will most likely be healthier for you. A co-worker of mine was buying her lunches at restaurants every day. The average meal with tax and tip was about $12-$15. She calculated that she was spending over $250 every month on lunches and the only thing she was gaining through it was weight. She made a decision to pack her meals. They were much healthier for both her body and her budget. The cost for making her lunches every day for an entire month was less than $100. In that one area alone she saved $150 per month. You will be surprised at how it adds up.

Grocery shopping

Plan your meals wisely and go to the store with a list. Purchase only what you need and always look at the comparative prices. Sometimes a certain brand will cost quite a bit more than another brand that might be just as good.

When you are tempted to purchase an item you normally would buy but realize that you don't need it, put it back on the shelf right away and move on. I had a friend who was a compulsive shopper. She never went to the store with a list and almost always shopped on her way home from work just before dinner. She never planned meals, so when she went grocery shopping she was hungry and bought everything that looked good. When I was helping her with financial management, I suggested that she should plan her meals before she went shopping, and go with a list.

One time after work she stopped by the supermarket to get a few items. She had not made a list that day. Her old habits were fully awakened as she walked into the store. She started filling her basket with everything that looked good. At the checkout she realized that she had stepped into her old pattern, so she decided to take out of the basket and buy only what she needed and to leave everything else. In her rough calculations, she realized that she had saved almost $100 in that one trip to the store. She had been spending an average of $600-$700 every month on groceries, but through proper management was now only spending around $300-$400. Some months she was saving $400 on food alone. That is almost $5,000 per year.

Also, buying only healthy food and carefully planning economic and tasty meals can create great savings.

Home utilities

Money can be saved on utilities. I have a friend who studied household energy conservation. She discovered that the electrical rates were lower at certain times of the day, so she planned her laundry and dishwashing around those times. She also adjusted the temperature of the house to economize. In the winter, she wore sweaters in order to use less heat and in the summer she used fans when possible rather than the air conditioner. The average utility bill for a home her size in her region is about $380 per month. She lowered her bill to under $200 at times.

Travel expenses

My husband and I live in a small community, and there are times that we cannot obtain what we need from what's available in our community. Since a larger shopping area is about a 50-mile round trip, we have saved on gas expense by waiting a day or two when possible and combining trips. This not only saves the gas expense but also the wear and tear on the vehicle.

Be strategic with your spending and make everything work toward a quality life for you. Ask yourself the big question again: "Do I really need this?" If you do in order to fulfill your financial goals and you have the money to spend, then go for it. You will be amazed at the extra finance you have when you are wise with your spending.

Faith

Faith is your connector to the promises of God. Choose to live in the realm of the miraculous and trust God for miracles and breakthrough. ONLY believe. Study the Word and when you find promises for provision, write them out and stand on those promises in faith. Remember them throughout your day. Meditate on them and BELIEVE! "If you can? All things are possible to him who believes" (Mark 9:23).

You do not need to live in the restraints of the natural realm. There is supernatural provision available for you. Always have an expectation for heaven to break into your realm in the earth. All of God's children have access to the blessings of God. "Your kingdom come, Your will be done, on earth as it is in heaven" (Matthew 6:10).

In the years when we struggled financially, I had very little money for groceries. I would go to the store with the little I had and pray for God to multiply it. As I walked up and down the aisles, I asked the Lord for His supernatural blessing and intervention. The Scripture says that when you seek, you find. I sought for sales and I found them. Every time I went shopping I would find items marked down, or sometimes land on a two-for-one sale. At those times I left the store with double and triple portions of what my money would normally be able to purchase. Think beyond the natural and believe for abundance and blessing.

Endurance and Patience

We live in a world where the expectation is to have everything NOW. It is through faith *and* patience that we inherit the promises (Hebrews 6:12). Good quality almost always includes the cost of patience. Lay hold of the promises of God and then endure, no matter what your circumstances look like. God's Word is true! When you lay hold of His promises by faith, do not grow weary while doing good; for in due season you will receive if you do not lose heart (see Galatians 6:9).

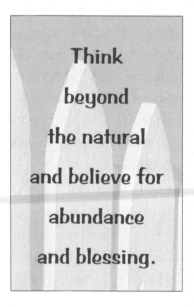

Think beyond the natural and believe for abundance and blessing.

During our difficult years, we stood on God's promises every day, and yet we often struggled to see the manifestation of what we believed for. We determined to stand on the truth and not waver. It paid off. Faith and patience are attributes that provide financial breakthrough.

Chapter 6

ROOTS OF POVERTY

AND LACK

Chapter 6

ROOTS OF POVERTY AND LACK

The axe is already laid at the root of the trees; therefore every tree that does not bear good fruit is cut down and thrown into the fire (Matthew 3:10).

A good tree cannot produce bad fruit, nor can a bad tree produce good fruit. Every tree that does not bear good fruit is cut down and thrown into the fire. So, then, you will know them by their fruits (Matthew 7:18-20).

If there is bad fruit, there is a bad root. When you destroy the *root* of poverty and lack, you will not see the bad *fruit* in your life. I experienced the pressure and temptation of lack and poverty years ago, although by the grace of God I kept the door closed to those spirits. Lack and poverty are definitely evil forces in the unseen realm and we must not partake of them. When God created man, He proclaimed blessing, multiplication, and abundance over him – not lack and poverty. You will not find lack and poverty in heaven, so you must not yield to these forces in the earth.

The Battlefield of the Mind

Your mind is where your conscious struggles begin. If your mind is focused on God and the truth of His Word, your life (including your finances) will be kept in perfect peace. Isaiah 26:3 says, "The steadfast of mind You will keep in perfect peace, because he trusts in You." Peace speaks of well-being, prosperity, deliverance, and salvation, and it is part of the nature of God.

When you are tempted, evil thoughts surface either from the carnal, fallen nature of man (James 1:14) or directly from the enemy. These evil thoughts release fear, unbelief, disobedience, and curses into an individual's life and launch a pathway of destruction. You can see this clearly in the account of Adam and Eve. The serpent came with evil thoughts that were contrary to God's Word. Fear, unbelief, disobedience, and curses were the results that continue to affect mankind to this very day. The battlefield was in their mind as they pondered what the serpent said. After pondering a while, they came into agreement with the lie and ate of it. This is when sin entered mankind. It all began in the mind.

We are taught in Scripture to watch over our heart (mind) with all diligence because from it springs the issues of life

(Proverbs 4:23). As a man thinks so is he (Proverbs 23:7). If you believe the lies of the enemy, those lies will create a root within your life.

I knew a woman who struggled with poverty constantly. The root of her problem was that she always meditated on her lack and how she never had enough. All day long, and even into the night, thoughts of lack and poverty plagued her. Instead of resisting them, firm in her faith, she entertained them. Those negative meditations became a stronghold that produced more negative results. When I would read promises for her financial well-being, she would say, "Yes, but..." She always had a reason why God's Word wouldn't work for her. She believed the lie of the enemy rather than the Word of God. Belief in the enemy's lies creates a landing strip for him to gain control. It is his welcome mat

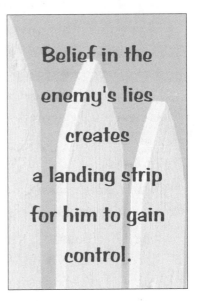

Belief in the enemy's lies creates a landing strip for him to gain control.

– his open door. And believe me, he will take full advantage of the invitation.

Ask Holy Spirit to convict you of any belief systems you adhere to that are not of God. Confess the sin of submitting to evil mindsets and invite the Lord to forgive you and cleanse you from all unrighteousness. Then, renew the mind with the promises of the Word of God. Fight using the Word of God. When a lie enters your mind, pull out your sword, the Word of God, and destroy the speculation that is not from the Lord. Cast down any thoughts that are contrary to the Word of God. Meditate on the truth and not the lie. My book, Decree, is a great tool to help you renew your mind. Another great help is to listen to the Scriptures. Various forms of audio presentations of the Scripture are available.

> For though we walk in the flesh, we do not war according to the flesh, for the weapons of our warfare are not of the flesh, but divinely powerful for the destruction of fortresses. We are destroying speculations and every lofty thing raised up against the knowledge of God, and we are taking every thought captive to the obedience of Christ —2 Corinthians 10:3-5

Generational Iniquity

When Moses went up the mountain to receive the Ten Commandments for the second time,

> The Lord passed by in front of him and proclaimed, "The Lord, the Lord God, compassionate and gracious, slow to anger, and abounding in lovingkindness and truth; who keeps lovingkindness for thousands, who forgives iniquity, transgression and sin; yet He will by no means leave the guilty unpunished, visiting the iniquity of fathers on the children and on the grandchildren to the third and fourth generations" —Exodus 34:6-7; also see Deuteronomy 5:9

It is possible for individuals to have a generational sin transference that has influenced their well being, as the sins are passed down to the third and fourth generation. This is one of the reasons why you often see similar patterns of lack and poverty in the generation line. The good news is that the generational iniquity can be forgiven and the pattern broken in the name of Jesus.

If you notice a curse of poverty that has come down through the generational line, repent on behalf of your forefathers for anything that has provided a landing strip for the enemy. Then receive forgiveness on behalf of them. Also, release forgiveness toward them from your own heart. After the slate is clean, then break the power of the curse in the name of Jesus. The following is a prayer you can follow:

Lord Jesus,

I stand in the gap for my generation line to the third and the fourth generations. I repent on my behalf and on behalf of my forefathers for any and every sin that has opened the door to poverty and lack. I ask that You forgive me and my forefathers for sinning against You. I receive forgiveness and cleansing from all unrighteousness according to Your Word in 1 John 1:9. I personally forgive anyone in my generation line who has transgressed Your Word and has brought harm to me and others that followed.

In the name of Jesus Christ, I break the power of the enemy's hold on my financial well being and prosperity. I break the power of the curses of lack and poverty.

In the name of Jesus Christ, I call forth the manifest blessing of abundance according to Your Word on my life and on the generations that follow, as I live and obey Your Word.

AMEN.

Wrong Teaching or Modeling in Childhood

The earlier you can learn good financial discipline, the better chance you have of living in established financial blessing. No matter your situation, it is never too late to change your ways.

Examine your financial failures and then determine what habit patterns opened the door. Look to your upbringing and reflect on the modeling you had. Identify specifics in the modeling that are not healthy for you. Make a list of those things so you can clearly identify the things that created bad fruit. Awareness is very helpful.

Then look for a good role model. Is there someone you know who is prosperous and who handles their money and financial dealings with integrity? If you have bad spending habits and financial management, get some good, wise, outside counsel and become accountable to them.

It will not accomplish much if someone gives you wisdom to create new spending habits but you ignore the advice. You are headed for another failure for sure. You will need to create new habits, and that takes discipline. Remember, if you keep doing the same things, you will get the same results no matter how much advice you are given or how many times you are bailed out.

If you are a parent, it is important to teach your children good spending habits early. My generation grew up in affluent times and many did not learn to curb their spending or plan well. It was easy to borrow or purchase on credit, so you had everything you wanted NOW. If your children wanted something, they got it. As a result, many of them did not learn the principles of responsible financial planning.

Find good role models and then become one.

Bad Spending Habits

This seems so obvious, but unfortunately it is the main root of poverty and lack – spending money you do not have or spending it on things that do not fulfill your financial goals. We have covered this previously, but it so important to admit to bad spending habits if that is indeed the issue. Take personal responsibility and implement change.

Unforgiveness

Bitterness, offense, and unforgiveness are killer forces. If someone has taken advantage of you financially and hurt you, it is very important to watch over your heart as you move forward. Unforgiveness will hold you in a prison of curse and lack. Receive healing and forgive. God is able to restore.

Murmuring and Complaining

Be careful what you confess with your mouth. Murmuring and complaining invites warfare. The Kingdom is full of encouragement and praise. Everything is good in God's realm and that is why there is so much joy in His presence. God works everything together for good, and there is joy in the lives of those who live in abundance. When you complain, you are stating that you do not believe God is good. You do not believe that He will cause you to triumph and bring you into a land flowing with milk and honey. Murmuring and complaining is a sign that reveals what your heart believes. It exposes unbelief.

Unbelief

Without faith you cannot please God (Hebrews 11:6). Faith is the connector to all God has freely given you through His promises. Unbelief and doubt will surely keep you from experiencing the blessings. In James 1:6-8, the Scriptures state that those who doubt are "like the surf of the sea, driven and tossed by the wind," and that a person who doubts should not assume that "he will receive anything from the Lord, being a double-minded man, unstable in all his ways." If you doubt, you are double-minded, and if you are double-minded, you will receive NOTHING from the Lord. You must believe!

Unworthiness

Sometimes individuals feel unworthy to live in abundance due to past failures, choices, or wrong indoctrination by certain religious teachings. Due to their perspective, they live a life bound by lack.

In the story of the prodigal son in Luke 15:11-32, we find a young man who grew up in a fairly affluent family. He made a demand on his inheritance prematurely. His father complied with his demand and issued to the son his full inheritance. The son went off and squandered the inheritance on sinful living. When it was all lost, he found himself empty, hungry, and completely broke. He attempted securing some work with a pig farmer for minimal pay, but then came to his senses. He thought, "My father's hired servants get treated better than this; I will return with an apology and ask him to hire me on as a servant." The prodigal son no longer felt worthy to be treated as a son due to his failures. His feelings of unworthiness caused him to see himself only as a hired slave in the house of his own father.

As he returned home, we find his father welcoming him as a son and treating him as a son. His identity was restored. His brother, however, did not agree with the father. He wanted to keep the brother in a lowly position, as he did not believe he was worthy to return as a son.

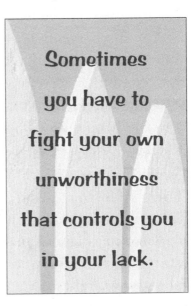

Sometimes you have to fight your own unworthiness that controls you in your lack. At other times, you have to battle against the opinions and judgments of others. The father of the prodigal son had the final say, and your Heavenly Father has the final say in your life. Your worthiness is found in Christ and not in your own works. When we fail and turn back to God, our worthiness to receive blessings is completely restored.

Negative Expectation

A woman expressed negative expectation to me one day by saying, "I just got a new job, but it probably won't last for long, just like the others." She proceeded to tell me how every time she secured a new employment opportunity it would terminate within a few months, and sometimes in a few weeks. She developed an expectation of failure. You will get what you expect.

After praying for another individual who was struggling financially, she said to me, "I'm not going to get my hopes up because I don't want to be disappointed again." Whoops! What a ditch to live in!

Yet another individual explained to me that they did not want to go out and find a job because they had been rejected by a number of companies they had submitted their resume to. They had an expectation that if they sought employment they would be rejected. And they were.

Take courage and break through the negativity barrier. Create positive expectation. I remember a salesman once told me that if he went to only five or ten houses a day selling their product, he might not sell anything. The key to his success (he was the top salesman in the company) was simple: he went to lots of houses. He went out each day with an expectation that he would make sales, and that is what he focused on. Instead of five or ten houses that might have given him a negative response, he kept going from house to house. Sometimes he visited 50 to 75 houses a day with an expectation that some of them would purchase his product.

He was motivated by his expectation. When one household shut the door on him, he went to the next one. He knew that at some point, someone would want his product, and if he went to enough homes, he would make a good living.

Years later he was called as a missionary to India. He used the same principle in preaching the gospel to a people who were resistant to it. He went from dwelling to dwelling and had many closed doors, but he knew that if he just kept going he would find someone who wanted the gospel. The first day he preached door to door, no one responded to him. The next day, he once again went from house to house and faced more rejection.

On the third day, a family invited him in. He returned the next day to that household and the entire family was saved. They invited their relatives and friends to study the Bible with them and there were many converts. This was his first church. Over the years he became a very successful missionary and planted many churches. He continued to sow the seed of the gospel with positive expectation. He KNEW that his persistence and positive expectation would produce results.

Laziness and Poor Work Ethics

Lack of diligence is certainly a root of poverty. " 'A little sleep, a little slumber, A little folding of the hands to rest,' Then your poverty will come as a robber And your want like an armed man" (Proverbs 24:33-34). I have met people that expect so much and yet invest so little. They want abundance, but they lack diligence. I have almost always seen diligent, faithful, workers blessed. There is no return on zero investment, and there is small return on small investment; but when you make a large investment you can expect great return for your labor.

I have met people with many dreams of abundance, but they do not have a consistent, healthy work ethic for implementing success. A young man I was mentoring a number of years ago had a difficult time getting up in the morning. He would sleep through his alarm and show up to ministry sessions late. This was a pattern he had walked in for years. He was fired from a number of jobs because of his failure to arrive on time.

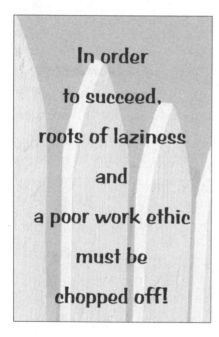

In order to succeed, roots of laziness and a poor work ethic must be chopped off!

A friend of mine who owns a coffee shop struggled with hiring employees who only fulfilled their work when someone reminded them what to do. This was laborious for management, so they fired such workers if they did not improve over time. Some of their employees were dishonest and stole from the shop by taking bags of coffee home. One employee even stole money from the cash drawer. This type of behavior will surely set you up for a poverty spirit. The money you save by stealing a pound of coffee or taking $10 from the cash drawer is not worth the long-term oppression of poverty you will live with as a result of opening the door to the enemy.

In order to succeed, roots of laziness and a poor work ethic must be chopped off!

Failure to Budget

Budgeting is very important for establishing financial stability and fruitfulness, as it will reveal what you need to believe for. When the Lord gives me a vision to fulfill, I plan a budget. I invite the counsel of God to reveal what is needed to fulfill every part of the mandate. I also pray for a strategy on how to raise the funds. Jesus taught us to "calculate the cost" before building (see Luke 14:28). It is easy for an expense budget to swell, and it is very surprising how little, wasteful additions can swallow up the funds. Budgets are to be stewarded in wisdom.

One time I was working on a project that was going to cost about $50,000 to fulfill. I had my expense budget in place, and by the grace of God was able to raise $38,000 toward the project. An individual became privy to the fact that we had $38,000 in the bank and suggested that we purchase a piece of equipment since we had the cash available. I had to explain that the money was designated for other purposes.

Budgets help you fulfill your financial desires and assignments. You cannot dip into funds allocated for one thing and spend them on another. You will end up with an unfulfilled assignment.

Good business practices include wise budgeting. This is also beneficial for your personal financial success.

Witchcraft Curses

I prayed for a family once who had ongoing, unusual financial disasters. Through a word of knowledge during prayer, we discovered a witchcraft curse. They explained they had some anger and frustration against a family member who had taken advantage of them financially in an inheritance situation years earlier (their anger and offense was the landing strip for the curse to land on). This family member was also involved in a witchcraft coven. It was discovered after the ministry session that this family member had literally placed an intentional curse on them through a destruction ritual.

After forgiving the family member, we immediately broke the curse through the power of the name of Jesus. There was an immediately breakthrough in their finances that continued to manifest over the next year. Their relative did not repent from witchcraft, but the victim was now a victor. We gave them confessions from the Word of God to proclaim over their lives so that they were no longer subject to curses.

You have power over all the power of the enemy and nothing will injure you! No weapon formed against you prospers (see Luke 10:19 and Isaiah 54:17).

The Love of Money

The love of money is the root of all evil according to 1 Timothy 6:10. God desires to bless us with money, houses, land, food, clothing, vehicles, and other things that we need in life, but we can never worship those things. When money is the love of our life and the motivating force that propels our choices, we are creating roots of poverty and lack.

God must be first, and things (including money) should be second. Jesus said to "seek first His kingdom and His righteousness, and all these things will be added to you" (Matthew 6:33).

Also, James 4:2-3 says, "You do not have because you do not ask. You ask and do not receive, because you ask with wrong motives, so that you may spend it on your pleasures."

Failure to Evaluate

As I've said before, if you keep doing what you have always done, you will continue to get the same results. A seasoned and successful businessman once told me that if a business is not experiencing a measure of success after the first two years of operation, it is important to evaluate the overall picture. He suggests in such a case that you call in a professional financial counselor or business advisor to evaluate the situation and provide some advice for improvement. He believes that if there is no sign of breakthrough after solid evaluation and implementation of the suggested changes, you should dissolve the floundering company. Through his years of experience, he has discovered that if there is not a sign of success after three years, there probably won't be.

Now, of course I believe that all things are possible with God and things can change for good at any time. We are not to give up on that which the Lord has revealed; yet there also needs to be some balance and practical wisdom in place.

I know a man who is very faithful and hard working, but he failed to evaluate his investment situation. He did not want to give up on his dream, but after many years there was still no sign of breakthrough. He was determined to win his battle, so he kept borrowing more and more money in order to sustain his investment. After a number of years, he lost everything. This could have been avoided if he had properly evaluated his situation and adhered to some of the outside counsel he was receiving.

In the multitude of counselors there is wisdom.

Destroying the Roots of Poverty

I have mentioned some possible roots of lack and poverty. Some of these might fit a situation you are in, others will not. No matter what the root is, it can be cut off.

To cut off the root, I recommend that you:

1. Determine what the root is.

2. Discover the landing strip that produced the root.

3. Receive forgiveness for any action or choice that produced a root.

4. Forgive others who were part of producing the root.

5. Invite the Lord to uproot.

6. No longer feed a root of poverty and lack. Fully repent (turn in the other direction).

7. Sow seeds of righteousness and wisdom that will produce abundance.

Take some time right now before the Lord and invite Him to reveal the roots and then remove them from your life ... forever!

Chapter 7

MOVING FORWARD

INTO ABUNDANCE

Chapter 7

MOVING FORWARD INTO ABUNDANCE

I t is time to move on – now! Not tomorrow or next week. Today! Do not be stuck in the failures of the past. You are going to move on into abundance. You can determine your glorious future by choosing to live in the truth of God's promises. Jesus came to give you an abundant life – this is the truth! Choose to live in the truth of His Word all the days of your life, no matter what your circumstances look like. Refuse lack and poverty! It might be a bit of a wrestle for a season, but you WILL win! It is worth the battle. Do not give up.

The following are some reminders for you as you step into your new life of abundance.

1. **Remember the Lord Your God.** Put God first in your life and honor Him by giving Him the first and the best of all you have. Bring your tithes and offerings before Him with a cheerful heart. Spend time in His presence and honor Him above all else. If you do not know Jesus as your personal Savior, invite Him into your heart by faith and ask Him to forgive you for all your sins. When Jesus becomes your Savior, all you are and all you have is His, and all He is and has belongs to you. It is not a fair exchange on His part, but it is the way He desires it. You can start a brand new life today by accepting Jesus as your Savior.

2. **Know Who You Are in Christ.** You are blessed and you are a blessing. You are a child of the God of Plenty. You are His covenant child and an heir of the promises. Always remember that you are a child of the King. You are in Christ and Christ is in you. The same glory the Father gave Jesus has now been given to you (John 17:22).

   When you meditate on who you are in Christ, you will over time manifest the fullness of what you have meditated on. Do not believe the lies of the enemy. Your thoughts and feelings can be deceptive, but the Lord's Word is true. For example, you might not feel like you are an overcomer, but the Scripture says that in Christ you are! The Word tells you who you are. Believe and prosper.

3. **Decree the Word.** The Word will not return void but will accomplish everything it is sent to do (Isaiah 55:11). When you decree the Word over your life daily, the manifestation of that Word will come upon your life. Decree the promises regarding provisional blessing and expect the manifestation. (You can purchase my *Decree* book online – see the advertisement in the back of this book for more information.)

4. **Love Wisdom.** With wisdom comes true riches and enduring wealth. Seek the Lord for wisdom in financial decisions. If you lack wisdom, ask for it and it shall be given (James 1:5). Be wise in your spending. The spirit of wisdom can also give you the knowledge of witty inventions and ways that you can produce wealth. Wisdom will help you create wealth and maintain wealth. Embrace wisdom.

5. **Plan Well.** Have a clear vision of your goals and a plan of action for fulfilling them. Without a vision you will perish, but with a clear vision and purpose you have a target for your faith. If you do not have a clear goal and plan of action, you will spin your wheels; but with good planning you can accomplish all your desires.

6. **Believe for Miracles and Supernatural Intervention.** Live with an expectation for the miraculous intervention of Christ and the service of His angels. You will encounter financial increase according to your faith. Believe and you will receive. Expect miracles,

blessings, and supernatural intervention and you will receive what you believe.

7. **Continuously Sow.** If you continuously sow, you will continuously reap. What you sow today you will reap tomorrow. Sow bountifully in good ground that will give you a strong return of blessing from the Lord.

8. **Create Multiple Avenues of Income.** Look for more than one avenue of income. For example, a young man I met shared with me about his full time employment position in media. He works around 37 hours per week on this assignment. He also has a small company in yard maintenance that he works at one day a week. He hires another worker part time to fulfill some of his other maintenance contracts.

His wife is at home raising children, but took a book-keeping course in order to help with their small yard maintenance company. She now has two clients in addition to their own business, and she has time for one more. She makes enough money each month through the bookkeeping contracts to cover their car payment. She also does some proofing for a publishing company every once in a while that gives them some extra spending money.

In addition to that, this couple rents out one of the rooms in their house. That rent brings in enough to pay for their utilities and phone bill. When you have multiple streams of income, you can ask for blessing and increase on each stream, and God WILL bless.

9. **Live a Life of Praise and Thanksgiving.** Thanksgiving offered to God for every good thing will open up realms of blessing for you. He is so good and faithful. Sometimes we forget to thank Him for all He has done. A good exercise is to take some time to write down all that you are thankful for. Be specific and don't leave anything out. As you meditate on the goodness of God, His presence will come and lift your attitude and perspective. Praise and thanksgiving is often the start of mighty victories in your circumstances (see 2 Chronicles 20:1-30). Remember to be thankful. Praise Him!

10. **Be Positive.** The Bible says that we should think on those things that are true, honorable, right, pure, lovely, and of good repute (Philippians 4:8). I was ministering to a woman at an altar one night and she shared with me a tragic situation that had happened in her life in the past. She explained that she had already received prayer, inner healing, restoration, and restitution, but she still wanted more prayer. She kept talking and talking and talking about the negative aspects of the situation.

The Spirit of God in me was disturbed. I finally questioned her, "You are now out of this situation and all has been restored. Can you set your mind on all the good things rather than reviewing the negative?" She could not hear me. She continued to explain the situation and how terrible it was, and was whimpering and whining. I could not get through to her.

She was stuck in the negativity. It was time for her to move on and set her mind on all the goodness of God. Unless she changes her attitude and perspective, she will invite more calamities into her life through her negative focus and meditation. If you are in this situation, move on! Do not be stuck in the past. Your future is bright!

It is Time to Step into Your New Beginnings

Your future is truly glorious. Old things are passing away and all things are becoming new. Your past failures are under the blood. Live in the glory of your new beginnings. You can do it! Cast down the old mindsets of failure and lay hold of all His promises concerning your life in His abundance. Live in the realm of His blessings the rest of your life.

Now it shall be, if you diligently obey the Lord your God, being careful to do all His commandments which I command you today, the Lord your God will set you high above all the nations of the earth. All these blessings will come upon you and overtake you if you obey the Lord your God: Blessed shall you be in the city, and blessed shall you be in the country.

Blessed shall be the offspring of your body and the produce of your ground and the offspring of your beasts, the increase of your herd and the young of your flock. Blessed shall be your basket and your kneading bowl. Blessed shall you be when you come in, and blessed shall you be when you go out.

The Lord shall cause your enemies who rise up against you to be defeated before you; they will come out against you one way and will flee before you seven ways. The Lord will command the blessing upon you in your barns and in all that you put your hand to, and He will bless you in the land which the Lord your God gives you. The Lord will establish you as a holy people to Himself, as He swore to you, if you keep the commandments of the Lord your God and walk in His ways.

So all the peoples of the earth will see that you are called by the name of the Lord, and they will be afraid of you. The Lord will make you abound in prosperity, in the offspring of your body and in the offspring of your beast and in the produce of your ground, in the land which the Lord swore to your fathers to give you.

The Lord will open for you His good storehouse, the heavens, to give rain to your land in its season and to bless all the work of your hand; and you shall lend to many nations, but you shall not borrow. The Lord will make you the head and not the tail, and you only will be above, and you will not be underneath, if you listen to the commandments of the Lord your God, which I charge you today, to observe them carefully. —Deuteronomy 28:1-13

A Decree for

Provision and Resource

From *DECREE* by Patricia King

I seek first the Kingdom of God and His righteousness, and all the things that I need are added unto me, for my heavenly Father knows what I need even before I ask. I do not fear, for it is my Father's good pleasure to give me the Kingdom.

I acknowledge that all my needs are met according to God's riches in glory by Christ Jesus. Grace and peace are multiplied unto me through the knowledge of God and of Jesus my Lord. His divine power has given me all things that pertain unto life and godliness, through the knowledge of Him that has called me to glory and virtue. Blessed be the God and Father of my

Lord Jesus Christ, who has blessed me with every spiritual blessing in the heavenly places in Christ. The Lord is a sun and a shield to me and will give me grace and glory.No good thing will He withhold from me as I walk uprightly.

I choose to sow bountifully, therefore I will reap bountifully. I give to the Lord, to His people, and to the needy as I purpose in my heart to give. I do not give grudgingly or out of compulsion, for my God loves a cheerful giver. God makes all grace abound towards me, that I always have enough for all things so that I may abound unto every good work.

The Lord supplies seed for me to sow and bread for my food. He also supplies and multiplies my seed for sowing, and He increases the fruits of my righteousness. I am enriched in everything unto great abundance, which brings much thanksgiving to God.

I bring all my tithes into the Lord's storehouse so that there is meat in His house. As a result, He opens up the windows of heaven and pours out a blessing for me so that there is not room enough to contain it. He rebukes the devourer for my sake, so that he does not destroy the fruits of my ground and neither does my vine cast its grapes before the time. All the nations shall call me blessed for I shall have a delightful life. I am blessed because I consider the poor. Because I give freely to the poor I will never want. My righteousness endures forever.

I remember the Lord my God, for it is He who gives me the power to make wealth, that He may confirm His covenant. Because Jesus Christ, my Savior, diligently listened to the voice of God and obeyed all the commandments, the Lord will set me high above all the nations of the earth and all the blessings in the Kingdom shall come upon me and overtake me. Christ became poor so that through His poverty I might become rich.

Jesus came so that I would have life in its abundance. I am very blessed and favored of God and have been called to be a blessing to others.

Scriptural References
Matthew 6:33; Philippians 4:19; Luke 12:32; John 10:10; 2 Peter 1:2-3; Ephesians 1:3; Psalm 41:1; 84:11; 112:1, 9; 2 Corinthians 8:9; 9:6-11; Proverbs 28:27; Genesis 12:2; Malachi 3:8-12; Deuteronomy 8:18; 28:1-2

Patricia King

Patricia King is president of Christian Services Association and XPmedia.com, Inc. She has been a pioneering voice in ministry, with over 30 years of background as a Christian minister in conference speaking, prophetic service, church leadership, and television & radio appearances. Patricia has written numerous books, produced many CDs and DVDs, hosts the TV program "Patricia King-Everlasting Love, and is the CEO of a number of businesses. Patricia's reputation in the Christian community is world-renowned.

Christian Services Association (CSA) was founded in Canada in 1973 and in the USA in 1984. It is the parent ministry of Extreme Prophetic, a 501-C3 founded in 2004 in Arizona. CSA/Extreme Prophetic is located in Maricopa, AZ and Kelowna, B.C. Patricia King and numerous team members equip the body of Christ in the gifts of the Spirit, prophetic ministry, intercession, and evangelism. CSA/XPmedia is called to spreading the gospel through media.

Author Contact Information

United States:
P.O. Box 1017
Maricopa, AZ 85139

Canada:
3054 Springfield Road
Kelowna, B.C VIX 1A5

Telephone: 1-250-765-9286
E-mail: info@XPmedia.com

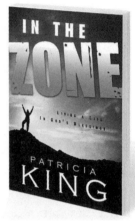
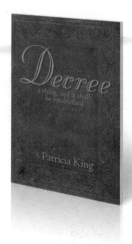

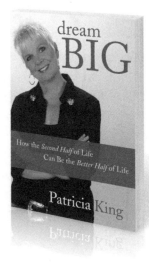
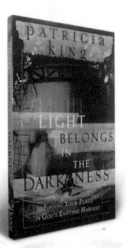

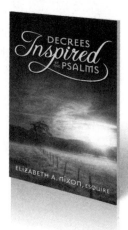

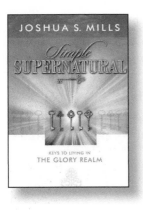
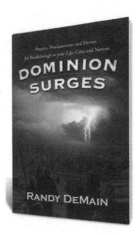

Additional copies of this book and other book titles from
Patricia King, and XP Publishing
are available at xpmedia.com

BULK ORDERS: We have bulk/wholesale prices for stores and ministries. Please contact usaresource@xpmedia.com and the resource manager will help you. For Canadian Bulk Orders please email resource@xpmedia.com.

www.XPpublishing.com
A Ministry of Patricia King and
Christian Services Association